NATIONAL
PLANNING
ASSOCIATION

Pensions for Public Employees

BY ALICIA H. MUNNELL

Vice President and Economist
Federal Reserve Bank of Boston

In collaboration with
ANN M. CONNOLLY

Research Associate, National Planning Association

With a Statement by the NPA Joint Committee
on Public Employee Pensions

PENSIONS FOR PUBLIC EMPLOYEES

NPA Report No. 171
Price $7.00

ISBN 0–89068–048–5
Library of Congress catalog card number 79–89303

Copyright July 1979
by the
NATIONAL PLANNING ASSOCIATION
A voluntary association incorporated under the laws of
the District of Columbia
1606 New Hampshire Avenue, N.W.
Washington, D.C. 20009

79-6955

Contents

Pensions for Public Employees

by Alicia H. Munnell
in collaboration with Ann M. Connolly

94 / Benefits for Hazardous Employment
95 / Problems Arising from Lack of Universal
Social Security Coverage
96 / Conclusions

99 / National Planning Association
100 / NPA Officers and Board of Trustees
102 / Recent NPA Publications

Tables

Preface

The establishment of a Joint Committee on Public Employee Pensions was authorized by the Trustees of the National Planning Association late in 1977. The purpose was to provide a means for a comprehensive identification of the basic issues and problems, both emerging and in prospect, regarding public-employee pension systems. Under the able chairmanship of John Macy and with the dedicated involvement of Hastings Keith as Vice Chairman and the strong support of John Miller as President of the National Planning Association, such a Committee was constituted early in 1978. Embodied in its diverse membership was a broad base of knowledge and experience in this field, along with intense interest and concern regarding many fundamental aspects of the subject.

On behalf of NPA's Trustees, I would like to pay a special tribute to the members of this Committee for the generous contribution of their knowledge, time and energies to the challenging and important task they agreed to undertake. The results have been the following: a Committee Statement entitled "Areas for Study and Issues for Analysis and Resolution" and the accompanying study on *Pensions for Public Employees,* authored by Dr. Alicia Munnell, Vice President and Economist of the Federal Reserve Bank of Boston, in collaboration with Ann Connolly.

It is NPA's customary practice that all active participating Committee members may sign the Committee Statement and to invite those who dissent to append footnotes. While a substantial majority of members did sign the following Statement, it should be noted that not all members of the Committee have signed. In particular, for various reasons some of the members representative of concerned labor-union interests did not wish to sign or to add footnotes.

It is hoped that the Statement and the accompanying study represent timely and useful contributions to increased understanding about the complex nature of many of the key issues arising in the field of public employee pensions. In particular, the effort to delineate and clarify these issues should be of special help in the context of other more intensive and specialized examinations of certain aspects of these matters now under way in other quarters.

I wish to express the special appreciation of NPA to:

●Dr. Munnell and to the Federal Reserve Bank of Boston for the contribution, without cost to NPA, of her time and efforts in this endeavor;

●The John Brown Cook Foundation for the initial "seed money" and a large part of the subsequent financial resources needed to bring the Committee's work to a successful conclusion; and

●The Ford Foundation and other private donors who provided complementary financial support vital to the Committee's achievements.

June 1979

Walter S. Surrey
Chairman,
NPA Board of Trustees

Areas for Study and Issues for Analysis and Resolution

A Statement by the
NPA Joint Committee on Public Employee Pensions

The accompanying report, by Dr. Alicia Munnell with the assistance of Ann Connolly, concludes that the public-employee pension problem is both large and complex; a concerted educational program is required to assure public understanding so that a climate can be created in which any needed reforms can be considered and adopted. In their concluding chapter, the authors offer a list of problems, options for reform and areas requiring further study. They point out that their list is not comprehensive, but rather serves to stimulate interest in a selected group of possible reforms.

The National Planning Association's Joint Committee on Public Employee Pensions, in the Statement that follows, presents a comprehensive listing of the problems, issues and main areas of study for the public-employee pension systems today.

The Committee views the development of a national policy for public employee pensions as the essential first step in addressing the wide range of subordinate issues involving public employee pensions. The President has recognized the need for a national pension policy and has appointed the President's Commission on Pension Policy to study this question. Too often the discussion on pension matters has focused primarily on the financial elements of the plans. The economic aspects and the fundamental role the plans play in our society are rarely considered. We are hopeful that the President's Commission will maintain the broad perspective that is required to develop pension policies which advance the best interests of retirees, the nation's workforce and society as a whole.

As a means of advancing the analysis and discussion process from which a pension policy can evolve, this Committee presents, as summarized below, a list of 12 areas for study and issues for analysis and resolution.[1]

The conclusions and opinions expressed in the following Statement are solely those of the individual members of the Committee on Public Employee Pensions whose signatures are offered hereto and do not represent the views of the National Planning Association or its staff. Committee members' disagreement with specific points of this Statement is expressed in signed footnotes.

1   The President, speaking before the Magazine Publishers Association on June 10, 1977, referred to the nation's pension system as, "the most horrible conglomeration of retirement plans that overlap and are wasteful and are sometimes unfair to deserving employees that you've ever imagined. It's shocking when you go into it."

The lack of a centralization of authority for pension matters within the Congress and similarly within the executive branch has fostered this "horrible conglomeration." There has been a proliferation of pension benefits as existing committees and their staffs tend to compete with each other in liberalizing the programs for the benefit of the retirees within their particular jurisdictions. Sound actuarial and accountability

(continued)

(1) How big should pensions be?

(2) What should be the relationship between retirement age and benefit entitlements?

(3) Should there be national standards for public-employee pension systems?

(4) What should be the response of public-employee pension plans to inflation?

(5) How should the costs be paid?

(6) How should public-employee pension plans relate to social security?

(7) What are the economic and social consequences of pensions?

(8) What is equity among retirees?

(9) Are present disability benefit systems satisfactory?

(10) How great a problem is "double dipping?"

(11) What are the transition problems as changes in the public-employee pension systems are discussed, designed and implemented?

(12) How should information about public-employee pension systems be collected and disseminated?

These 12 areas for study and issues for analysis and resolution are each discussed briefly below, together with suggestions for the types of study in each area which would best contribute to the public policy discussion. The Committee is aware of an increasingly wide range of study activity in the pension field. To the extent that any of those efforts overlap into these 12 areas, then this Committee suggests early circulation of the study results. Otherwise, the Committee hopes to encourage such studies in the future.[2]

(Footnote 1 continued)

techniques are not the routine responsibility of these committees. They are almost incidental to their main work.

The Comptroller General has recommended that the responsibility for pension legislation be centralized in one committee (one for the House and one for the Senate). The Chairman of the Civil Service and Post Office Committee has indicated an interest in this concept. Such consolidation would provide a focal point for the consideration of the broad spectrum of factors that must be recognized in the formulation of a national pension policy, both public and private.

The creation of this congressional committee structure would be a tangible, understandable first step toward implementing such recommendations as the President's Commission on Pension Policy proposes. These committees of the House and Senate would similarly be the proper agencies to consider and act upon such studies as flow from Dr. Munnell's report and this Committee Statement.

It is regrettable that the chances of the Comptroller General's recommendations being acted upon favorably are very slim unless public support for such a change can be generated. Consolidation of congressional jurisdiction of pensions should be, in my opinion, the top priority in the list of areas for study and resolution set forth by the Committee.—**Hastings Keith**

2   There have been many studies conducted of military compensation and pensions—most recently the President's "Commission (ZWICK) on Military Compensation." It concluded its work on April 28, 1978. Its recommendations are strikingly different from those of earlier studies. The Commission's recommendations are now being reviewed by the executive branch. I believe they will shortly be sent to the Hill for consideration. The users of Dr. Munnell's report and of the Committee Statement should study the ZWICK report.

It recommends, for instance, that those who retire early should not receive a full pension after 20 years. They would, under the ZWICK Commission, get a somewhat smaller pension (at an earlier age

(continued)

THE COMMITTEE AND ITS PURPOSE

The National Planning Association has had a continuing interest in the pension area. In 1952, Robert M. Ball wrote an NPA report for the Joint Economic Committee entitled *Pensions in the United States*. In 1977, the work of the NPA Joint Policy Committee on Private Pensions culminated in its report and statement, *The Role of Private Pensions in Maintaining Living Standards in Retirement* by Robert Clark. NPA extended its activities to the public-employee pension area with the creation of the present Committee which was charged as follows:

> . . . the structure and financing of our public-employee pension system is becoming an increasingly important national issue which can best be resolved in the public interest if it is approached comprehensively and not piecemeal, as at present. . . . We believe a comprehensive overview is required. . . . The Joint Committee, with the aid of professional staff, will be asked to develop at this time a comprehensive study design which will describe all the major aspects, problems and issues of the public pension systems which should be examined in depth.

The Committee effort is timely, given the rising level of general interest and the start of major studies by a number of federal advisory bodies. It is the hope of this Committee that its overview can be helpful in these and other efforts.

In assembling the Committee, NPA Vice Chairman (and former NPA President) John Miller, Committee Chairman John Macy, and Committee Vice Chairman Hastings Keith gathered a diverse membership representing groups with an interest in public employee pensions as well as previous experience with public-employee pension problems. The Joint Committee obtained the services of Alicia Munnell, Vice President and Economist of the Federal Reserve Bank of Boston, as its Research Director; Dr. Munnell drafted the accompanying report in collaboration with Ann Connolly. Rather than presenting policy recommendations, that report and this Statement focus on the information that must be obtained and the still extremely controversial issues which must be resolved in order for beneficial and widely accepted policies to be considered, adopted and implemented.

Many public employers originally offered job security and future retirement benefits in place of higher wages. But today, pensions are more often conceived as a part of total compensation which should allow a career public employee to acquire benefits during her or his working life permitting a comparable standard of living after retirement. This intent of providing economic security has been extended in many cases to protection against disability as well as protection for survivors in case of untimely death.

Many of the public-employee retirement systems of today were instituted several decades ago. Now they need to be examined to determine the extent to which they

---

(Footnote 2 continued)

than at present) until such time as they completely retire. In short, they would work longer in the military or in the private sector and then get their full pension at a more normal retirement date—and it would be more appropriately related to social security.

These recommendations are most worthy of study by those researching the question of early retirement for all circumstances.—**Reginald J. Brown**

still meet the needs of their participants and beneficiaries, and of society at large. Many factors have changed since these systems were first instituted: people are living longer; more families have more than one income; high inflation rates erode benefits and complicate pension planning. In some cases, retirement system benefits designed to stand alone have been augmented by social security. Retirement systems designed for a different time and for different socioeconomic conditions may need to be redesigned, and the whole pattern of retirement and its funding appears to need reappraisal in the light of changed conditions and needs.

A pattern of pension plans has developed which is not comprehensive and which differs significantly at federal and at state and local levels. While some public employees are well protected, serious gaps in coverage and benefits for other public employees still exist. Yet, there is a growing question of the effect on budgets and the economy of the cost of public pension plans, including social security.

SPECIFIC ISSUES FOR
ANALYSIS, STUDY AND RESOLUTION

The Committee offers the following list of 12 areas deserving thorough consideration.

(1) How big should pensions be? The purpose and role of retirement and other pension benefits need clarification, to aid in balancing their justification against the cost of different levels of protection. Some specific issues are: (1) What part of total compensation should pension costs represent? (2) Should any part of the provision for retirement be left to the individual? If so, under what circumstances?

How should total compensation be divided between (1) current income, (2) medical, vacation and other current benefits, and (3) future pension benefits? From the management and taxpayer points of view, pensions are a significant element in total compensation, and a key part of a benefit package intended to increase motivation, loyalty and productivity.

For the employee, a pension plan can represent a degree of economic security for old age, against disability, or for survivors in case of death. After retirement, the cost of continuing a comparable living standard has been estimated at about 80 percent of final average salary at lower income levels and about 60 percent at higher income levels, on an inflation-protected basis and including all income sources. In some cases, there are additional costs for survivors of employees. What sort of continuation of level of living should be the objective for public-employee pension systems? Should the objective be the same for all public employees?

Study. The key study area concerns a more careful determination of (a) the cost of pension benefits including inflation protection; (b) the degree to which existing plans provide specific benefits; and (c) the location, nature and cost of the gaps to be closed.

(2) What should be the relationship between retirement age and benefit entitlements? Some of the issues surrounding retirement age and benefit entitlements involve clarification of: (1) what retirement is, in terms of employment and lifestyle alternatives; (2) a separation between (a) early retirement as a career change, with immediate start of benefits or with a vested pension payable at a later time, and (b) early retirement as a form of disability pension or as an employment incentive; (3) consideration of the degree to which delayed retirement should bring larger

benefits; and (4) the potential impact of increased longevity on the public-employee pension systems.[3]

Early retirement options, long a routine feature of uniformed-service pension plans, have spread to other public and private plans. Except for some of the service plans, these options have been tied to actuarially reduced benefits until recently. Pensions can be planned for retirement at any age, but the cost of the options needs to be related to the pension financing, especially since some of the existing early retirement plans are very costly.

What improvements can there be in pension and employment planning for employees in assignments which require that they be removed from work in mid-career? This may occur either because these employees have become disabled or because the normal aging process disqualifies them from continuing to meet the job demands. Where the individual is injured by the employment exposure, a disability-type pension seems obvious. In the case of a career shift for a normal individual no longer able to meet very special job demands, is a pension to be preferred over continued employment and reasonable job progression? However, where continued employment is not possible, some have suggested partial pensions as an alternative to a full retirement pension before normal retirement age. And extra pension incentives may be deemed necessary to attract individuals to unusually hazardous or demanding employment (such as police, fire fighting, military).

With the federal legislation enacted in 1978, retirement of most employees cannot be required for reasons of age before age 70 in the future. Compulsory retirement for reasons of age has been abolished for federal employees; its abolition elsewhere has been proposed and will be very seriously considered. Thus, later retirement as well as early retirement may become major considerations in public-employee pension planning.

For persons who are still able to obtain income sufficient for their needs from other sources, should there be incentives for delaying the start of pension benefits?[4]

Study.   The study in this area would deal with the implications of different definitions of retirement; whether pension entitlements should be affected by a job change, a shift to part-time work, or retirement out of the workforce; and how pension benefit schedules and continuing employment should relate to each other at different retirement ages.

(3) Should there be national standards for public-employee pension systems? How could reasonable benefit standards be defined for (a) retirement, (b) disability and (c) survivor benefits, as an aid in comparing plans and developing benefits to a reasonable level of adequacy? Are such standards possible? Would they be useful?

---

3   *And (5) should consideration also be given—for demographic and "productivity" reasons—to the possibility, even probability, that the services of experienced though aging persons will be increasingly in demand—with many technological "assists" to facilitate the use of full-time or part-time employees or managers with waning physical stamina—so that delayed retirement incentives can be used both to promote this trend and decrease the drain on retirement funding?*—**Robert F. Woodward**

4   *Some retirees are both willing and able to work. Considering the frequent questions about whether the national economy can sustain a truly adequate living standard for all retirees in the future, it seems supremely important that all who want to work be given an incentive to do so, in a way that partially relieves the strain on current retirement benefit payments.*—**George C. Sawyer**

Would they be enforceable for state and local governments by federal legislation? Have they been attempted in other countries? What should be the specific purpose of each type of benefit (full support versus supplement to other income)? Should top-income employees receive pensions based on the same formula as for lower-income employees, or should pensions be based only on income up to some pre-determined level? Should employees at certain income levels be expected also to have private savings in order to continue their full living standard after retirement?

PERISA (a Public Employee Retirement Income Security Act analogous to ERISA, which established fiduciary and administration standards for private-sector pension plans) apparently will be a serious proposal. How similar are the needs for such legislation in the public employee area? How serious and how widespread are the reported managerial problems with some public-employee pension plans; that is, due to absence of reporting and disclosure standards, or fiduciary violations such as conflict of interest, or improper control of pension operations, or improper political influence? What is the extent of employee participation in the management of public plans? What is the extent to which plan information is disclosed and reported to employees and to the taxpaying public?

What would be the impact of an established uniform retirement policy for all federal employees? What problems would it create or eliminate? Is there another way of eliminating the problems where the various plans fail to fit together smoothly?

To what extent are vesting standards needed for public-employee pension plans? Vesting comes only after 20 years of service in the military, and later in some state and local plans. Under some plans, employees leaving before vesting lose their contributions; under other plans, those leaving after vesting has been achieved and who obtain a refund of their own contribution thereby forfeit the vesting of the employer contribution; even with vesting, there is generally no protection against inflation from the time of leaving that employment until retirement. Lack of vesting tends to restrict employee mobility; hence, even from the employer's point of view, how desirable is it to retain employees who stay only because they cannot afford to sacrifice pension benefits?

Occasionally, public-employee pension plans make possible benefits that exceed basic preretirement earnings. Alternately, some career public employees do not have adequate benefit levels. The need is to correct the system where necessary; for example, to raise benefits where they are inadequate, to provide earned benefits lost for lack of vesting and portability protection, or to modify disability benefit formulas if they discourage return to productive work.

Study.   The necessary study would consider whether national standards are desirable and possible. The issue will be over the wisdom, utility and practicality of making such standards specific, and whether they would apply to the federal service or also include state and local plans. If inclusion of state and local plans seems desirable, what are the constitutional and legal questions? Proposals such as PERISA could be examined from the perspective thus developed. Appropriate benefit standards might also be studied although they are unlikely to be specified in legislation relating to nonfederal plans.[5]

---

5   *Granting the desirability of a PERISA, the study should review the high administrative costs reportedly experienced under ERISA*—**Kenneth J. Kelley**

(4) What should be the response of public-employee pension plans to infla-tion? Pensions have traditionally been based on the premise that the inflation rate would be moderate enough so that postretirement benefit increases would not be essential. Historically, however, even moderate inflation has significantly eroded the purchasing power of pensions. Presently, the outlook may be for higher than historical inflation rates. The impact of inflation on the purchasing power of a fixed income is shown in the following table.

**Effect of Inflation
on Pension Purchasing Power**

Average Annual Inflation Rate	Pension % Lost	Purchasing Power after 15 Years % Remaining
0%	0%	100%
3	37	63
5	54	46
8	72	28
10	79	21

Thus, as these figures indicate, a worker retiring today at age 65 on a fixed pension could expect to have between two-thirds and one-fourth of today's purchasing power remaining at age 80, depending on whether the United States is successful in bringing inflation back to the lower range of past experience. But, is it socially acceptable that pension purchasing power be allowed to fall to half or less of the planned level?

Benefits paid by social security and federal pension plans are now indexed; that is, adjusted to maintain the purchasing power of the pension as the value of the dollar declines. Some state and local pension plan benefits are at least partially indexed.

With improvements in health and lifespan, many retired people can expect to live 15, 20 or even 25 years after retirement. As the proportion of older voters in the population increases, the loss of purchasing power would have become an acute issue in any case. Inflation has averaged 3 percent per year since the American Revolution, and if recent experience were to continue, it would suggest a future rate of 5 percent or more.

Pensions based on income continuation and income security objectives will require protection against loss in purchasing power. To the extent that pension payments are not adjusted to keep pace with cost-of-living increases, this will be a retreat from these two objectives, although some believe that such a retreat may be necessary.

Study. The policy issue is the degree to which public employers will affirm and extend protection of pension benefits against erosion due to cost-of-living increases in the face of the cost of such protection. The key study areas concern the cost of such extension, its possible economic impacts, and the consequences in terms of alternatives for paying the cost.[6]

(5) How should the costs be paid?   Pensions are often considered as a form of deferred compensation for present employment, but how they should most appropriately be financed may differ for private, federal and state and local plans. Past practice, as illustrated by ERISA's requirements for private pension plans, has been to require that the full cost of future benefits be made a part of current wage and salary expense, and invested under proper supervision to provide a fund sufficient to guarantee the payment of benefits when they become due. Are different standards appropriate for state and local plans and for federal plans?

The initial cost of pension benefits varies greatly according to the relationship between initial benefit level and preretirement income, retirement age and past service requirements. It also varies because of actuarial assumptions and the actual experience of the plan as to longevity and the management of the portfolios.

The cost of pensions is substantially increased where benefits are adjusted to keep pace with rising living costs. Where reserves are being set aside, indexing increases their required size, and also requires a complex series of adjustments as actual inflation rates differ from those assumed in the basic calculations for the plan.

Pay-as-you-go plans provide the payments to retirees as a current expense burden at the time that the payment is due. Other plans are only partially funded. Some have objected to this type of financing as leaving this generation's debts for another generation to pay. The problem is different for state and local governments than for the federal government. Pay-as-you-go was rejected for private firms by ERISA because of the many cases where the firm ran out of money or went out of existence, and the retirees were left without pensions. Government units are less likely to go out of existence, but the sharp escalation of pension payments has already caused acute pressure on tight budgets.

Where financing of public-employee pension plans may be inadequate, the risk of unmanageable tax burdens or benefits in default is created. Necessary benefit increases in some of the plans which do not provide adequate retirement income levels would only increase financial pressures. Better information is needed on the present level of funding, together with year-by-year projections of the increasing retirement benefit commitments for the different categories of public employees, plus identification of the areas where the stability of the governmental financing and pension systems are in greatest jeopardy. A major public policy issue will arise over where the money is to come from.

Study.   An appropriate study of this area would start by collecting or developing projections of the future pension benefit costs year by year for individual public-employee pension plans as compared with scheduled contribution income augmented by investment income from any reserves set aside for this purpose. For the major federal plans, many of the funding issues have already been considered. The emphasis would be much more on the state and local plans, their present and prospective methods of funding, and reporting and disclosure of plan information. Then, from an overview of the cost problem that the financing of present policies

---

6   *The study area should include data on the extent of protection against inflation provided in state and local public employees' plans—i.e., indexing and caps if any.*—**Kenneth J. Kelley**

and commitments represents, the issues of how best to pay the cost can be better defined and studied, with the size of the problems and the nature of the solutions likely to be different for the many different types of public-employee pension plans.[7]

(6) How should public-employee pension plans relate to social security? Present social security coverage of public employees is uneven, with 25 to 30 percent of state and local employees and nearly all federal civilian employees not covered. Of those not covered, some employees have some of the forms but usually not the scope or level of protection that social security gives to the rest of the population. Employees who move in or out of social security coverage may lose protection; or government retirees may get social security benefits after minimum service.[8]

Under these circumstances, can an optimum relationship between social security and the public-employee pension plans be achieved by extending social security coverage and designing public-employee pension plans to be supplementary to social security? Or can it be achieved by some other kind of relationship? Are there limits to federal authority or other legal barriers to prevent restructuring of federal-employee pension plans or state and local plans? What can or should be done about any limits or barriers?

If social security coverage were to be made universal for all public employees, what changes would be necessary in existing pension plans, and what would be their consequences? Alternatively, if social security coverage is not extended to public employee groups, would statutory changes be needed to limit either gain or loss of benefits when an employee changes employment and moves in or out of social security coverage?

Study. The need here is for a careful fact-finding and analytical study to examine the issues arising out of the relationship between social security and the public-employee pension plans, and the costs and consequences of possible changes.

(7) What are the economic and social consequences of pensions? Retirement provisions, disability standards, provisions as to vesting and portability, and other features of pension systems influence the national style of life. Are the incentives created by pension provisions consistent with the types of living patterns the United States wishes to encourage among contributing and retired workers and their families? What will be the effect on marriage and the family unit? How will active and retired employees find their lives influenced?

Many of the so-called abuses of pension plans arise because someone has found a way to turn the regulations to personal advantage; this is neither illegal nor

---

7   *This study will point up the degree to which state and local plans are unfunded or inadequately financed. The Proposition 13 syndrome will exacerbate the problems.* **—Kenneth J. Kelley**

8   *In my opinion, the uneven coverage of public employees by social security involves serious equity problems which deserve more emphasis in this type of statement. Public employees who are not covered are relieved of the social responsibility (imposed by law on covered employees) to contribute to the cost of provisions which weight the benefit formula in an effort to provide "socially adequate" pensions for beneficiaries with low average lifetime earnings from covered employment. On the other hand, the beneficiaries of public-employee pension plans who meet the minimum requirements for social security benefits, often through part-time or postretirement work, can get substantial advantages from the weighted aspect of the benefit formula and the method that is used to compute a retiree's earnings from covered employment.* **—W.E. Hamilton**

improper. How frequent and how costly are these instances? Should the nature and scope of these provisions be reexamined and suitable adjustments considered? Or are the social and economic impacts of the public-employee pension systems sufficiently consonant with their intended objectives?

What is the impact of pensions and pension indexing on public employer budgeting and financing? What are the political and social consequences of pensions and indexing? To what extent do pensions contribute to inflation when they represent unexpected or uncontrollable cost increases? If retirees receiving assured pension income change their saving and spending habits as a consequence, what are the economic and social consequences of any such changes?

A number of social issues have been raised over the investment of pension funds. (1) Should these funds be invested in a particular region to facilitate its development, even at some sacrifice in return? Or are fiduciary responsibility and maximum income the primary investment criteria? (2) What is the consequence if the funds are invested in the securities of the employer (e.g., New York City)? (3) What impact does the investment of these major funds have on today's society?

Study.   Most of the individual issues seem to have both economic and social dimensions and both need to be more clearly delineated. The necessary studies might start with the the analysis of the impact on the economy and society of how pension costs are paid, contrasting the impact of indexed and nonindexed pensions with full, partial or no funding at the time of employment and the balance of the cost paid out of current funds when benefits are due. Next would be the economic and social impact of the form chosen for pension investments;[9] that is, federal securities versus securities of other kinds, or investments tied to regional development or support of a specific government. The final and perhaps most profound level would be the sociological and economic impact on the way that individuals and groups adapt their lifestyles in response to the constraints and opportunities defined by the pension systems. The first task at all three levels would be factfinding and analysis to determine what the impacts now are, and what the possibility is for alternatives with better impacts.[10]

(8) What is equity among retirees?   As one aspect of the commitment to equal opportunity, retired citizens may more and more tend to expect comparable benefits from comparable employment. To the extent that gross inequities exist, with some pensions large and others small in relation to past earnings, and to the extent that some pensions are protected against inflation and others shrink away with the passage of time, a controversy may arise.

The "gray power" movement is only one manifestation of the more activist posture of today's older people, and the trend is for the degree of activism to

---

9   *In an inflation-racked society such as ours, government securities and other traditional pension investments are highly vulnerable to loss of value. A safe inflation-protected investment vehicle is badly needed. Few alternatives have yet received serious consideration. Because the investments lose value against inflation, rather than compounding as in the past, future pension benefits are doubly hard to fund.* —**George C. Sawyer**

10   *It seems inappropriate to include in this all embracing category, with diverse economic and sociological factors, such an item as the investment policies of pension funds. This item more properly should be located under 5 or 11.* —**Kenneth J. Kelley**

increase in the future. Demographic projections show the coming rapid increase in the numbers of elderly, who seem likely to be active voters. Also, retirees will have the sympathy of the older members of the labor force and others who think about their own retirement.

Potent political opposition seems likely for any proposal perceived by the elderly or retirement-oriented fraction of the nation as representing a serious threat or injustice to old and retired people. Such issues seem likely as the disparity between retirement benefit levels increases.

The extremes will be between those with meager fixed-income pensions (particularly those without social security) versus the retirees from good, fully indexed public employee plans supplemented by social security. With the possible continuation of higher-than-historical inflation rates, the indexed and nonindexed retirement incomes will diverge rapidly in purchasing power from year to year.[11]

Study. The key study area concerns (a) the actual degree and scope of the disparity between retirement benefits for similar types of employment, and (b) the degree and scope of the disparity due to full indexing or partial indexing as opposed to no indexing of supplemental retirement benefits, in the light of present and prospective social security payments for the eligible and any special problems of the ineligible.[12]

(9) Are present disability benefit systems satisfactory? Are present disability plans providing the intended coverage? To what extent do public employee groups still lack this protection? How can the increasing cost of disability benefits be managed and moderated to keep the necessary costs within the bounds of possible budget and taxpayer support?[13] Why are disability costs rising? Disability benefit costs have been increasing faster than other pensions costs; what can or should be done?

Should disability standards written around the performance of one specific assignment be used as a measure of employability or unemployability? Should workers be classified and compensated as disabled for life even though recovery may occur? Partial compensation for partial disability or for the need to shift to other employment has been suggested, as well as partial reduction of disability payments as recovery occurs; could these or other concepts improve the system?

---

11   *As inflation continues at 5, 7 or 13 percent per year, as the case may be, the value of any fixed income will be eaten away to the point that the best hope of many elderly will be to die before their income becomes too small to live on. The contrast with those on fully indexed pensions will be dramatic, and is likely to bring acute political stress. This could bring pressure for massive increases in social security, lessening the need for other pensions and savings. Or it could bring pressure for other alternatives equally difficult for the national economy to sustain.* —**George C. Sawyer**

12   *The "gray power" potential impact can be better understood if the percentage of the population over age 65 is stated for 1960, '70, '80, and '90.* —**Kenneth J. Kelley**

13   *It seems to me important in this connection to point out that the increasing incidence of disability under the social security program rose during the early '70s but reached a peak in 1975 and has since been declining. In 1978, the number of new claims approved was roughly 460,000 as compared to 600,000 in 1975. The social security disability insurance system, at least, seems to be under good control.* —**Robert M. Ball**

Is it reasonable that the majority of some employee groups retire on disability pensions? Do such circumstances suggest a serious problem either in working conditions or disability plan administration? What is the actual reason for some of the high disability retirement rates reported? Are definitions of disability in the various public-employee pension plans satisfactory?

Study. The appropriate study would start with a review of the variety of disability plan standards, administration and experience; this would provide a background for considering some of the many suggestions for changes in disability benefit plans. Then the most promising alternatives would be defined and analyzed for impact, cost and policy implications. This could result in a report summarizing policy alternatives and suggesting the types of action consistent with specific public policy objectives.

(10) How great a problem is "double dipping?" What exactly is "double dipping?" Or, more broadly, (1) is it possible to get benefits beyond those intended in the design of a particular pension system and beyond those needed for a reasonable standard of income continuation? (2) How extensive are any costs to the pension systems from such benefits? (3) Is remedial action necessary?

Study. An appropriate study would seek the answers to the above questions together with the costs or savings and the policy implications of potential changes.[14]

(11) What are the transition problems as changes in the public-employee pension systems are discussed, designed and implemented? The size and success of the present public-employee pension systems create a massive and proper self-interest of all of the enrolled individuals; how can their rights be understood and respected as needed changes are made? Because of the complexity of these pension issues, analysis of specific proposals for changing the pension systems seems to be the only way to discover fully the extent of the present interests. Many changes in public-employee pension systems have been suggested. These include proposals for universal social security, a common federal pension, and legislated standards for public-employee pension plans.

Study. The study in this area would begin by reviewing or completing the analysis of the above and other major proposals for changes in the public-employee pension systems, as well as any logical alternatives to them. From this analytical base it would then be possible to summarize some of the key elements which must be considered in the transition from the present as any changes in the public employee pension systems are designed and evaluated.[15]

(12) How should information about public-employee pension systems be collected and disseminated? With the growing number of groups actively studying the pension systems from various points of view, the need is growing for organization of the information exchange so that duplication of effort is minimized. Then, as the public policy issues inherent in any proposal for change in the public-employee

---

14   *To the extent possible, the degree of "double dipping" should be put in perspective since it stigmatizes all public employee pensions.*—**Kenneth J. Kelley**

15   *An essential ingredient for change should include actuarial valuations of state and local plans. During transition, a formula for freezing unfunded liability at present levels plus normal costs is developed.*—**Kenneth J. Kelley**

pension systems come into discussion, the gathered information could be made available, both in response to inquiries and in some more outgoing effort, to assist in public education so that individuals and groups can select and advocate the policy they may wish to support as the public policy debate moves toward consensus.[16]

Study. The necessary study would define the public-employee pension information needs and the potential roles of some of the active groups, and then suggest some of the mechanisms by which the necessary clearinghouse and information functions could be performed.[17]

FOR THE FUTURE

The purpose of this effort by the Joint Committee on Public Employee Pensions of the National Planning Association has been to provide an overview of a complex

---

16   *During the time that this Statement and the Munnell report were being written, many additional efforts to study the public-employee pension systems surfaced. The Joint Committee's staff uncovered literally dozens of studies of various aspects and elements of public pension systems—many of them government funded. A variety of studies are also under way under the auspices of business, labor, various associations of retired people, and others. It appears that thus far there has been no organized method of keeping track of these projects so that their knowledge could be shared and duplication of effort could be avoided. There is a need, therefore, to establish a clearinghouse to collate and disseminate all the work in this field.*

Together with the clearinghouse and the informational service it could provide, an organization should be established to safeguard the public interest and conduct research. Hopefully, it would be financed by foundations and staffed by personnel selected with the public interest paramount. To avoid suspicion of institutional bias, individuals and groups with known special interest would not be encouraged to participate.

I am also concerned that despite the serious nature of present problems in the public pension sector, general recognition of these at the technical level and a plethora of previous studies (for example, at least five major studies of military retirement), very little fundamental corrective action has been taken. Most responses have been patchwork changes which have often compounded the problem and the costs—while leaving basic problems untouched. Ideally, a fail-safe monitoring system should be adopted to ensure that the public has timely notice of impending pension problems, before they require emergency action. The need is urgent, and the record of the past is not encouraging.

The task before us now is to alert the general public to the emerging pension crisis and the need for reform. In so doing, it is necessary not only to present the problem(s), but to offer specific, achievable solutions.

The members of those supporting—and in most cases profiting from—the status quo are alert and aggressive. They are well organized minorities. The implications of their efforts, socially, politically and economically, must be understood in order to get the public interest and support that is necessary for pension reform. Important incremental changes in existing pension programs consistent with good public pension policy are possible. They can be advanced, debated and enacted if the climate for reform can be created.

If it becomes evident that more fundamental changes in public pension policy are called for (e.g., universal social security coverage or major restructuring of social security), the public participation in timely incremental changes will help to generate the climate needed to win support and understanding of the more fundamental and substantial reforms. **—Hastings Keith**

17   *Effective organization and dissemination of information about public employee pensions is essential to secure the public impetus necessary to effect corrective changes. This should be comparable to the Hoover Committee reorganization efforts of a generation ago, with a national committee and committees on state levels focusing on their respective jurisdictions.* **—Kenneth J. Kelley**

problem by utilizing the views of a group with members familiar with many of the specific pension issues and, by design, diverse enough to attempt to look at the whole problem. With the President's Commission on Pension Policy, the Advisory Council on Social Security, the National Commission on Social Security, and the Department of Health, Education and Welfare study of universal social security all in early phases of their activity, the public policy debate that can lead to consensus and implementation of public employee pension system changes may now be starting. It has been the hope of this Committee to contribute to that process through the present effort, as well as through the future interests and efforts of NPA and of the various Committee members.

Considering that wise changes and politically possible changes in systems as complex as those for public employee pensions most often come in small increments, the opportunity to encourage the next step in these necessary incremental changes may be approaching. A contribution toward the achievement of any improvement would fully justify past and present efforts. All concerned should bend their efforts toward moving these pension issues forward out of the discussion stage, to aid in developing a public policy consensus and pressing toward its implementation.[18,19,20,21,22,23]

The Committee commissioned Dr. Alicia Munnell of the Federal Reserve Bank of Boston and author of numerous publications including *The Future of Social Security*, in collaboration with Ann Connolly, to prepare the report which this Statement accompanies. The report provides an overview of the public pension systems, outlines controversial policy issues, describes a few policy alternatives which are designed to provoke thought, and discusses some areas in which future study is needed. Dr. Munnell assumes responsibility for this report. Without necessarily endorsing all of the findings and conclusions therein, the Committee approves its publication as a valuable contribution to public and governmental understanding of the important public-employee pension policy issues.

---

18   *In regard to the issue of universal coverage or "integration" of social security and other public pensions, it is difficult if not impossible to make a definitive statement on a proposal not yet formulated.* — **Betty Duskin**

19   *During the depression of the early 1930s, my congressional district suffered from unemployment which, as I recall, reached higher than 30 percent. During those years, the considerable differences of the status of the public employee with his relatively more stable income and employment naturally resulted in some hostilities between him and the private citizen whom he served.*

Today's industrial society—dependent as it is upon questionable supplies of energy—is much more vulnerable to changing economics and changing moods—than the relatively stable, largely rural society of the '30s. The potential hostilities between the public and private sectors could be even more in the 1980s than they were in the great depression.

I believe bringing common sense into total compensation (considering not only pensions, but job security) as we used to do is essential, even urgent.

I and, I believe, the other members of the Committee are glad for the opportunity to have helped in this report and Statement. I hope the public will respond to the challenges of this problem and support the Congress in its efforts to provide sound pension policies for all Americans. —**Brooks Hays**

20   The Committee Statement is implicitly involved with the Munnell report and, therefore, the questions posed are shaped, in part, by biases which I reject. I preceive them to be:

- *universal social security is more a solution than a problem;*
- *the purpose of criteria of adequacy is to identify the rare excesses in benefits rather than to expose widespread deficiencies;*
- *standards of adequacy may be different for the private economy and public employment, and the government response to "excess" may differ as well;*
- *data drawn from the federal civil service, the military and the large cities are relevant to thousands of smaller state, county and municipal systems.*

Future studies would benefit from different perspectives. —**Terry Herndon**

21   In general, I am in agreement with those who feel that action is called for at this time rather than further research and exploration into the nature and magnitude of the problems of pensions, including both the social security system, the public-employee pension plans, and the voluntary plans in the private sector. I will limit comments to two areas.

First, with respect to disability benefits, there has been a general awakening to the heavy financial cost of disability benefits in the social security system and in some of the public retirement plans. Some corrective measures have already been taken. However, in addition to the financial burden there are even more important social considerations. All too often the issue in the individual case is whether a person is legally or technically entitled to benefit payments. This results in countless contests between individuals seeking the income and administrative and adjudicative establishments seeking to avoid illegal payments and to contain the cost of benefits.

To a large extent, the situation has developed out of history and tradition. The tradition of paying disability benefits or pensions stems from commendable humanitarian motives. It predates by many centuries the development of modern medicine, current knowledge of health preservation and the techniques of rehabilitation. The latter generally date back only to World War I, since when the medical specialization of physiatry and the great advances in physical and occupational therapy and in vocational training and retraining have occurred. However, the financial rewards held out to the inidividual who qualifies for disability benefits have removed or greatly reduced the disabled person's motivation to take advantage of these rehabilitative services.

What is needed is a completely new attitude toward disability, one which puts primacy on medical restoration and, where needed, vocational rehabilitation. To overcome the ingrained thought patterns which militate against this positive approach, the term permanent-total disability should be expunged from our vocabulary, and no commitment involving the payment of cash benefits over a long period of time should be made or even discussed until all possibilities of functional restoration or rehabilitation have been fully explored.

The second issue which I wish to mention is that of universal social security coverage. The many vexing problems of public retirement systems and inequities among the various forms of employment or self-employment could best be overcome, in my opinion, by a very simple structure under which all workers would be brought into the social security system. Supplemental programs of an employer-employee nature, or maintained by self-employers, would be subject to the minimal necessary regulation and proper integration with social security through a single set of laws and regulations governing all supplemental retirement programs, regardless of whether the employer is an individual, a corporation or a unit of government or governmental authority. In short, there would be no discrimination among employees and other workers by reason of the kind or status of employment. —**John H. Miller**

22   The basic report by Dr. Munnell brings together a very significant amount of information about the problems confronting public-employee retirement systems (PERS). The Committee Statement suggests a number of important priorities as to study areas. However, I believe the situation with regard to PERS is so serious and the solutions so evident that more forthright and immediate recommendations for action should be made.

The blunt fact of the matter is that, on the whole, the benefits provided by PERS are overly costly and extravagant. The true test is that such benefits could not be afforded economically for the remainder of the nation's workforce. The retirement ages in PERS are unduly low (and could not be afforded by the nation as a whole for social security and private pensions plans) and the benefits when combined with

(continued)

(Footnote 22 continued)

those of the social security system (either provided directly along with those of the PERS or indirectly by the individuals obtaining social security coverage on the outside) are excessive, frequently being well above net take-home pay.

It is not so much further studies that are needed, but rather action to correct these glaring excesses. The changes needed are both within the PERS themselves and within the social security system so that universal coverage is achieved and all persons have the desirable basic floor of social security protection upon which reasonable supplementary protection can be built. In my opinion, studies of broad economic effects are of no value or significance because it is impossible ever to make such measurements (because changing one element produces unknowable effects on many other elements which have their own significant effects).

If any studies are to be made, they should be in the areas of determining how many beneficiaries under PERS are actually not retiring but working elsewhere and in determining the validity of the claim that the provisions of PERS cannot be modified for current employees, even with regard to future service. It is, of course, logical and equitable that accrued rights should be preserved, but there is no reason why such savings clauses should apply to benefits based on future service, any more than salaries and positions are guaranteed. If there are any legal provisions or court decisions that seem to yield this result, studies should be made as to how they can be legally changed.—**Robert J. Myers**

23   *The Statement of the Committee and Dr. Munnell's report serve a useful purpose by assembling an impressive volume of information bearing on public-employee pension systems. However, the list of issues would serve a more useful purpose, in my opinion, if it distinguished between issues in need of further study and those that are ready for action. For example, except for the transitional problem, additional study of whether social security should be extended to government employees seems unnecessary. Study means delay, and unnecessary study serves those who oppose change.*

The Statement also fails to deal adequately with the question of whether the overly generous benefits of some government plans should be more consonant with those of private-sector plans. On this latter point, I offer the following observations.

The statement of issues seems to imply that government plans will continue to set their own standards, presumably on the theory that it will be up to the private sector to close the gap that currently exists. But, it is apparent to many observers that the generous benefits of the federal pension system are already too costly to duplicate for other workers.

Many also believe that the private pension system should set the standards for public plans. They point out that private plans are more responsive to the disciplines of competition, cost considerations and funding. They also meet the statutory requirements of ERISA.

On the other hand, government plans are free from many of these restraints. As a result, they can and do defer the funding of future liabilities. Thus, the true costs of pension commitments are obscured until they impact on future generations of taxpayers.

Should government pension plans be reformed as a singular system, without regard to nongovernment plans? This is the threshold issue. Since the statement does not squarely raise it, one is left with the impression that in the future it will be equitable and economically appropriate for a government to guarantee a continuation of the standard of living enjoyed by its employees at the time of retirement when this ideal may be beyond the capability of businesses in the private sector, many of which are not only answerable to stockholders, but must also maintain a financial capability to compete in the marketplace.—**Eugene M. Thoré**

Members of the NPA Joint Committee on Public Employee Pensions Signing the Statement

JOHN. W. MACY, JR.
Chairman; Director Designate, Federal Energy
Management Agency

*THE HON. HASTINGS KEITH
Vice Chairman; Former Member of Congress

*ROBERT M. BALL
Senior Scholar, Institute of Medicine, National
Academy of Sciences

*REGINALD J. BROWN
Former Staff Director, President's Commission on
Military Compensation

VARY T. COATES
Associate Director, Program of Policy Studies in
Science & Technology, George Washington
University

JOHN J. CORSON
Former Director of the Bureau of Old Age and
Survivors Insurance

ROGER E. DAHL
Director, Labor-Management Relations Service,
U.S. Conference of Mayors

DAN. H. DAVIDSON
City Manager, City of Austin, Texas

*BETTY DUSKIN
Director of Research, National Council of Senior
Citizens

THOMAS C. EDWARDS
President, TIAA-CREF

GEORGE ELSEY
President, American Red Cross

ORVILLE L. FREEMAN
Former Secretary of Agriculture; President and
Chief Executive Officer, Business International,
Inc.

KENNETH A. GIBSON
Mayor, City of Newark, New Jersey

*W.E . HAMILTON
Chief Economist, American Farm Bureau
Federation

*THE HON. BROOKS HAYS
Former Member of Congress

*TERRY HERNDON
Executive Director, National Education
Association

RAY HOLBROOK
County Judge, Galveston County, Texas

HAROLD K. JOHNSON
U.S. Army, Retired, Former Chief of Staff

*KENNETH J. KELLEY
Former Deputy Director, Office of Labor Affairs,
AID, Department of State; State Coordinator,
Concerned Seniors for Better Government

GEORGE MADDOX
Director, Center for the Study of Aging, Duke
University

*JOHN H. MILLER
Consulting Actuary, Suffield, Connecticut

JOHN D. MILLETT
Vice President and Director, Management
Division, Academy for Education Development

*ROBERT J. MYERS
Professor, Actuarial Science, Temple University

JAMES J. O'LEARY
Vice Chairman of the Board, United States Trust
Company

JAMES G. PATTON
Former President, National Farmers Union

---

*See footnotes to the Statement.

JEROME E. ROSOW
President, Work in America Institute, Inc.

*GEORGE C. SAWYER
President, Management Technology and
Resources; Associate Professor of Management,
Hofstra School of Business

CI IMILLE I. CCI IOTTLAND
Dean, Heller School, Brandeis University

*EUGENE M. THORÉ
Attorney, Washington, D.C.

WAYNE E. THOMPSON
Vice President, Environmental Development,
Dayton-Hudson Corporation

CHARLES L. TROWBRIDGE
Senior Vice President, Bankers Life Company

*THE HON. ROBERT F. WOODWARD
Former Ambassador

Dr. Alicia Munnell, who prepared the accompanying report, played an active and valuable role as a member of the Joint Committee on Public Employee Pensions. However, since she is an author of the study which follows, she is not a signer of the Committee Statement in keeping with NPA's normal practice.

Acknowledgments

We would like to thank members of the National Planning Association's Joint Committee on Public Employee Pensions for extremely useful comments and suggestions. Sharon Davis provided capable research assistance in preparing the original draft, and Jennifer Katz contributed substantially to the revisions. Anna Estle was primarily responsible for typing and overseeing the production of the various drafts. Geraldine Hollman graciously provided additional secretarial assistance. Alicia Munnell is grateful to Frank E. Morris, President, and Robert W. Eisenmenger, Director of Research, of the Federal Reserve Bank of Boston for providing time and support in order to prepare this study.

1

Introduction and Overview

Public employee pensions are complex institutions which play an important role in our economy. Public pension benefits not only represent a major source of retirement income for government employees and constitute an integral part of the compensation package with which governments attract qualified personnel, but they also represent a significant financial obligation for taxpayers who pay the major portion of pension benefits. Today, the growing cost of public retirement plans necessitates a careful evaluation of their structure as well as of their success in achieving their goals at the least possible cost to the taxpayer. This type of careful study hopefully will be as useful in preventing indiscriminate benefit cuts in the wake of Proposition 13 fever as in correcting any excessively generous or inadequate benefit practices.

Dispassionate and thorough scrutiny of public plans is essential because, unlike private firms, governmental units have not operated in a competitive environment where profit maximization is the only requirement for survival. In contrast to the private manager who is motivated to minimize costs in order to show a profit, the public-sector counterpart is primarily motivated to satisfy the needs of the public.

In meeting these needs, public-sector managers at the federal level and sometimes at the state level are constrained by taxpayer resistance and by the principle of "comparability" in the amount of wages and salaries they can offer prospective employees. Adherence to the comparability principle attempts to ensure that public-sector wages and salaries are set at the level of the wage prevailing in the private sector for similar work. However, this principle has been difficult to extend to pension benefits. Hence, the major countervailing force operating against over-compensation in the pension area is the public's resistance to tax increases.

While taxpayers immediately feel the effects of increased wages, they may not be aware of increases in compensation provided through liberalization of pension benefits because of the deferred nature of retirement obligations. Unless rigorous funding practices are employed, the burden of pension costs for current employees can easily be shifted from the current to future generations of taxpayers. Because future generations are rarely the relevant constituency of current public officials, the discipline of public accountability is undermined.

Even when legal mandates for funding exist, the full fiscal impact of statutory funding requirements may be easily evaded by plan administrators who adopt overly optimistic actuarial assumptions. By underestimating the costs of future benefit payments, employers may reduce current pension obligations without appearing to transgress legal requirements.

The convenience of underfunding provides an opportunity for fiscal laxity. Rather than making difficult and sometimes unpopular tradeoffs within the budget, officials may borrow effortlessly from future taxpayers to finance overruns in the current operating budget. Consequently, in such cases it has been relatively easy for public-sector managers to accept employee demands for increased pension benefits without risking cutbacks or disruptions in services to the public. Recent taxpayer concern and activism may cause public-sector managers to change this behavior.

Even when pension costs are translated into tax increases, the public may fail to identify public pensions as the source of the increase. Although the total cost of pension benefits represents a large portion of the total budget, incremental benefit changes are frequently small in relation to the total budget. When these expenses are spread over the entire taxpaying population, the increment in tax rates attributable to a particular benefit liberalization is likely to be minimal. More visible budget items with larger tax consequences, such as educational or welfare expenses, tend to be the focus of public scrutiny. As a result of the dilution of costs, benefit liberalizations are less likely to be closely monitored even when full funding standards are followed.

The absence of strict accountability to taxpayers for benefit liberalizations and accruing pension expenses eliminates pressure on elected officials for containment of these costs. On the other hand, unionization of public employees has created a vocal constituency advocating benefit increases. Whether directly through the collective bargaining process or more often indirectly through lobbying efforts directed at the legislature, unions exercise influence on the design of pension provisions. When employee pressure for liberalization in pension benefits finds little taxpayer resistance to cost increases, cost escalation is the usual consequence.

In view of the political environment in which public pensions operate, an informed electorate is the most powerful mechanism for ensuring that these plans provide an adequate retirement income for public workers and an incentive to attract high caliber personnel at the lowest possible cost to the taxpayers. To improve understanding of the public pension area, this study summarizes the existing information as it pertains to the major issues in the public plans. Emphasis has been focused on the overall level of compensation for public employees compared to their counterparts in private employment; the financing and funding practices in the public sector; the lack of portability of pension credits within and between governmental units and between public and private employment; the special issues raised by those in hazardous employment; and, finally, social security coverage for excluded public employees. The study concludes with a summary of the major problems and selected policy options—highlighting those areas where further information or research is required.

As an introduction to the study, the following sections briefly summarize the major characteristics of the public pension system.[1]

DEVELOPMENT OF PUBLIC PLANS

Public pension plans have experienced explosive growth during the last 15 years.

---

1   For a more complete description of these plans, see Robert J. Myers, *Social Security* (Homewood, Ill.: Richard D. Irwin, Inc., 1975); and Robert Tilove, *Public Employee Pension Funds* (New York: Columbia University Press, 1976), pp. 9–11.

Table 1–1.   Number and Membership of Public-Employee Retirement Systems of Federal, State and Local Governments, 1975

Level of Government	Number of Plans	Membership (thousands)		
		Active	Nonactive	Total
State and local	6,630	10,387	2,347	12,744
Federal (uniformed services)	4	2,181	1,094	3,275
Federal (nonuniformed services)	64	2,839	3,402	6,241
Total	6,698	15,417	6,843	22,260

Source: U.S. House of Representatives, Committee on Education and Labor, *Pension Task Force Report on Public Employee Retirement Systems,* 95th Cong., 2nd sess., March 15, 1978, p. 59.

This expansion reflects the enormous increase in employment as a result of a greater demand for government services, increasing government salaries, rising rates of inflation, and the emergence of strong public employee unions—particularly at the state-local levels.

Federal, state and local government pension plans are as varied as they are different from private plans. As of 1975, there were 6,698 public pension plans, including 6,630 state and local government plans and 68 federal plans (see Table 1–1). The state and local plans covered about 10.4 million full- and part-time workers, and another 2.3 million were receiving benefits or were eligible for deferred benefits. Of the 68 federal plans, the two largest—civil service and military retirement systems—accounted for 4.8 of the 5.0 million active members. The remaining 66 systems had about 183,000 active employees or about 5.6 percent of the total active membership in all federal plans.

Historically, the first public-employee retirement system, covering the police force in New York City, was established in 1857; this predates the earliest private plan which was founded in 1875 for the employees of the American Express Company. Many additional municipal plans were created during the last half of the 19th century, including a number of systems for teachers. In 1911, Massachusetts developed the first state system to cover its general government employees. Prior to World War II, some states adopted retirement systems, but the major development occurred between 1941 and 1947 when 22 states enacted pension plans. Today, the vast majority of all state and local government employees participate in a staff retirement plan of some kind.[2]

At the federal level, military pensions date from the Revolutionary War when veterans and their surviving spouses were provided payments for disabilities which

2   For a discussion of evolution of state-local pension systems, see Thomas P. Bleakney, *Retirement Systems for Public Employees* (Homewood, Ill.: Richard D. Irwin, Inc., 1972), pp. 1–9.

Table 1–2.   Social Security, Veterans and Public Employee Programs: Cash Benefits, 1976

Program	Total	Retirement	Disability	Survivor
	Amount of Benefits (millions)			
Social security	$75,332.1	$48,069.0	$ 9,965.6	$17,297.5
Federal employees	16,524.6	12,761.1	2,535.0	1,227.7
Federal civil service	8,563.4	5,884.7	1,564.2	1,114.5
Armed forces	7,673.7	6,638.4	936.7	98.6
Other federal	287.5	238.0	34.9	14.6
Veterans programs	8,409.2	0.5	6,147.4	2,261.3
Railroad retirement	3,570.4	2,147.1	420.8	1,002.5
State and local	7,700.0	6,685.0	565.0	450.0
	Number of Beneficiaries (thousands)			
Social security	32,564.0	20,624.3	4,523.6	7,416.1
Federal employees	2,600.5	1,726.8	440.8	432.8
Federal civil service	1,432.0	759.0	279.3	393.7
Armed forces	1,131.8	940.1	156.1	35.6
Other federal	36.7	27.7	5.4	3.5
Veterans programs	5,456.5	0.4	3,235.4	2,220.7
Railroad retirement	1,025.7	587.2	100.8	337.7
State and local	1,840.0	1,580.0	110.0	150.0

Sources: Social Security Administration, Office of Research and Statistics, "Benefits and Beneficiaries under Public Employee Retirement Systems, Calendar Year, 1976," Research and Statistics Note #8 (Washington, D.C., July 11, 1978), Table 1, p. 4, and unpublished data; and Social Security Bulletin, Vol. 41 (March 1978), Table M–13, p. 47.

reduced their earning capacity. The plan for civil service employees was enacted in 1920. Originally, the plan was quite modest, without survivor protection or vested deferred benefits.

CHARACTERISTICS OF MAJOR PUBLIC PLANS

The following sections briefly describe the nature of today's major public retirement systems and the role they play in the provision of retirement, disability and survivor protection.

Civil Service Retirement System

Virtually all civilian federal workers are covered under the civil service retirement system. As of 1976, the civil service system paid $8.6 billion in retirement, disability and survivor benefits to 1.4 million beneficiaries (see Table 1–2). The system is financed by contributions from employees and the employing agency paid to a retirement fund which receives interest from government securities in which it is invested, plus an appropriation from general revenues. A summary of the main features of the system's benefits, financing and reserve position follows.

Benefits. The civil service retirement system provides retirement, disability and survivor pensions and also lump-sum refunds for those separating from service. Full retirement benefits are payable under several combinations of age and service: age 55 with 30 years of service, age 60 with 20 years (or 10 years service as a member of Congress), and age 62 with 5 years. Full disability benefits are payable after 5 years of service. The definition of disability is considerably more liberal than is social security's; the civil service awards benefits to individuals who are unable to perform the duties of their usual occupations while the social security requires that the individual be unable to engage in any substantial employment. Survivor pensions are provided for widows, widowers and children of active workers, regardless of their dependency. After retirement, survivor pensions are provided automatically for children, but only for nondependent widows or widowers if the pensioner takes a reduced annuity. This reduced annuity, which is usually referred to as a joint and survivor benefit, is equal to 55 percent of the full pension for which the retired member was eligible (i.e., before the deduction for the survivor protection premium).[3]

The basic employee pension or annuity depends on the number of years of service and the average salary during the highest 3 consecutive years. The general benefit formula is 1.5 percent per year for the first 5 years, 1.75 percent per year for the next 5 years, and 2 percent per year thereafter up to a maximum pension of 80 percent (attained after 42 years of service). Both the retirement annuities and survivor benefits are increased automatically twice a year to reflect accumulated changes in the consumer price index. Specific groups such as law enforcement agents and members of Congress have special formulas.

Disability pensions are calculated with the same formula as retirement pensions, except that a special minimum, usually 40 percent of the high 3-year salary, is provided for those with short service (but with at least the 5 years required for eligibility purposes). The minimum provisions are applicable for disability cases with less than 22 years of service.

Financing. Each employee contributes 7 percent of his base salary and the employing agency makes a matching contribution to the civil service retirement disability fund. In 1971, the Treasury Department began to make additional payments to meet most of the remainder of the overall cost of the program. As a result of the 1969 reforms, Treasury began to transfer amounts equivalent to an increasing proportion of the interest on the unfunded liability (10 percent in fiscal 1971, 20 percent in 1972, and so forth) and by 1980 will be paying all of the interest on the accrued unfunded liability. In addition, Treasury makes annual level payments to amortize over a 30-year period any increase in the unfunded liability resulting from any statute

---

3   Myers, *Social Security*, p. 575. Actually, the reduction required is small relative to the actuarial cost of purchasing such additional protection. The first $300 of monthly pension is reduced by only 2.5 percent and all pension above this amount is reduced by 10 percent. This compares favorably with the true actuarial cost which averages about 15 percent.

enacted after October 20, 1969 which authorizes new or liberalized benefits, extension of coverage or increase in salaries on which benefits are based.

In fiscal 1975, total contributions to the civil service fund amounted to $9.2 billion. This amount, which included the 14 percent from the employee and employing agency and the Treasury interest payments, totaled to 26 percent of payrolls. By 1980, after the phasein of the interest payment on the unfunded liability is completed, costs as a percent of payroll will amount to almost 33 percent. As of 1975, the fund held assets of $38 billion.

Military

Members of the military services are covered by a noncontributory plan, which is operated on a completely pay-as-you-go basis. Pension benefits are awarded after 20 years of service regardless of age (with Congress' consent) or unilaterally with 30 years of service. Except in the case of disability, no benefits are provided for those who leave with less than 20 years of service. The retirement benefit is calculated on the basis of 2.5 percent of final basic pay for each year of active service up to a maximum of 75 percent. However, because basic pay excludes allowances for subsistence and housing as well as special pay, a person retiring with 30 years of service at a benefit rate of 75 percent receives a pension equivalent to about 50 percent of the final total annual compensation.

Joint and survivor benefits of 55 percent of retired pay are provided on an elective basis as under civil service. However, unlike civil service, survivor benefits are integrated with social security. The military service benefit is reduced by the portion of the spouse's OASDHI benefit which is attributable solely to military coverage under OASDHI.[4] Both retired retainer pay and survivor benefits are automatically adjusted twice annually for accumulated changes in the cost of living.

State-Local Pension Plans

State and local pensions have grown rapidly in the last 15 years. This growth reflects the enormous increase in state and local employment and the influence of strong public employee unions. During the 1960–75 period, membership in state-local pension plans increased from 4.5 million to 10 million, and the proportion of full-time employees covered by such plans now stands at 90 percent.[5]

At the time of the Pension Task Force census,[6] there were 6,630 independent state-local pension plans of varying size, each with its own eligibility, vesting, fi-

---

4   The survivor benefit is offset by payments made under Dependents Indemnity Compensation, which are benefits for survivors of members dying of active duty causes.

5   U.S. House of Representatives, Committee on Education and Labor, *Pension Task Force Report on Public Employee Retirement Systems*, 95th Cong., 2nd sess., March 15, 1978, p. 59.

6   Congress established the Pension Task Force in the 1974 ERISA Act to undertake a comprehensive study of federal, state and local public-employee retirement systems. In 1978, the House of Representatives Committee on Education and Labor completed the study by surveying 96 percent of all public pension-plan participants.

nancing, and benefit provisions. Plans vary not only by state, but also within states and localities where frequently there are separate plans or systems for general employees, teachers, police, fire fighters, legislators, and judges. For instance, within the state of Pennsylvania alone, there were over 1,400 different plans. Furthermore, while most state and local employees are covered by social security, coverage is not universal. Although approximately 85 percent of general state employees have social security coverage, only 36 percent of the members of police and fire plans have such coverage. Teachers (other than those in higher education) are less likely to be covered, 56 percent, than are other local government employees.[7]

While the characteristics of state and local plans are diverse and complex, it is possible to describe features of what might be considered a "typical" plan. Robert Tilove, in a study of state-local retirement systems, surveyed a large number of plans and summarized the following characteristics of a typical plan for general employees covered by social security.[8]

Benefit formula: each employee's annual pension is calculated on the basis of 1.67 percent of the final salary for each year of employment. Therefore, after 30 years of service, the benefit would be equivalent to 50 percent of final salary. Final salary is defined as the average of the 5 highest paid years in the last 10 years of service.

Postretirement adjustment: pension benefits are increased annually, up to 3 percent, in line with changes in the consumer price index.

Retirement age: employees may retire with full benefits at age 60 with 10 years of service, and actuarially reduced benefits are available at age 55. Retirement is compulsory at age 70.

Vesting: if an employee leaves after 10 years of service and does not withdraw accumulated contributions, that individual is entitled to benefits at the appropriate age.

Disability: disability benefits of not less than 25 percent of final average salary are provided to workers with 10 years of service. The service requirement is waived if the disability is job-connected.

Survivor benefits: retiring employees can elect a reduced benefit for themselves in exchange for survivor benefits for their spouses.

Employee contributions: the employee contributes 5 percent of pay; if the employee terminates employment, a refund with interest can be obtained.

Social security: the employee's state-local benefits generally are not reduced to account for social security coverage.

In short, the typical employee of state or local government after 30 years of service can retire at age 60 on a pension of 50 percent of average pay for the last five years. In addition, like other workers, the employee can draw full social security benefits at age 65, which increases the pension income to about 80 percent of final salary.

---

7   *Pension Task Force Report*, Table B–7, p. 59.

8   Tilove, *Public Employee Pension Funds*, pp. 9–11.

Table 1-3.   Comparison of State-Local, Civil Service and Military Retirement Plans

Characteristic	Retirement System		
	Civil Service	Military	State-Local
Age and/or service for retirement	Age 55 with 30 years	20 years of service	Age 60–65 with 20–30 years of service
Calculation of benefit	1.5 percent first 5 years 1.75 percent second 5 years 2 percent for years over 10 Maximum: 80 percent of salary	2.5 percent per year of basic pay Maximum: 75 percent of basic pay	1.5–2 percent per year of service
Base for calculating benefit	High 3	Terminal basic pay	Basically high 3–5 years
Cost-of-living adjustment	Automatic	Automatic	Automatic adjustments are common; generally limited to 3 percent
Vesting	After 5 years	20 years	After 5–10 years
Social security offset	None	Survivor benefit only	About 70 percent of employees are covered by social security; 25 percent provide an offset or step rate formula with fixed-dollar integration level
Employee contribution	7 percent of salary	None	More than 90 percent are contributory: 3–8 percent of salary
Funding	Partial	Pay-as-you-go	Partial

Source: Defense Manpower Commission, *Defense Manpower: The Keystone of National Security,* Report to the President and the Congress (April 1976), Table VII-13, pp. 370–372.

Summary

The main characteristics of the three major pension systems are summarized in Table 1–3. For general state-local employees, the retirement age is between 60 and 65, although police and fire fighters can retire considerably earlier. For federal civil service, retirement age is around 55, while in the military the retirement age is the early 40s. The calculation of benefits in all three cases is quite similar: a designated percent of final salary for each year of service. The military and civil service adjust benefits by the full cost-of-living change while the state and local plans that do provide cost-of-living increases limit them to 3 percent.

The financing of the three systems varies significantly. State and local employees covered by social security pay about 5 to 6 percent, while those not covered contribute 7 to 8 percent. Civil service requires a contribution of 7 percent which contrasts sharply with the noncontributory financing of the military retirement plan. Furthermore, the military is financed on a pay-as-you-go basis and has no assets, while both state-local and civil service make some contribution toward funding their systems.

2

Public Pension Benefits

Pension plans operated for the employees of federal, state and local governments represent a major source of retirement income for government workers as well as a significant financial obligation for taxpayers. Public pension benefits have grown significantly, and the increased costs of these plans—because of inadequate pre-funding, demographic shifts and inflation—have become a subject of general concern. Moreover, the tendency for taxpayers to perceive public pension benefits as more generous than those in the private sector has stimulated public inquiry and in some cases resentment.

Pension benefits, however, are only one component of a total compensation package and therefore cannot be the only criteria used to compare public and private employees' compensation. For example, higher pensions in the public sector may offset lower public employee salaries. Since pension benefits are best evaluated in the context of the total compensation package, this chapter explores the available data on the relative wages and pensions in the public and private sectors.

WAGES IN PUBLIC AND PRIVATE EMPLOYMENT

In the private sector, wages are established by the activity of market forces. However, government employers, operating outside the marketplace, are less influenced by the interplay of supply and demand when determining the wages they should offer to attract qualified personnel. In order to provide a logical basis for the construction of a competitive pay scale, federal government employers have adopted the principle of comparability. This means that public-sector wages and salaries are set at the level of the wage prevailing in the private sector for similar work. At the federal level, the principle of comparability is strictly applied in a formal wage adjustment process; most states have informally adopted this approach, and it is used irregularly by cities and towns.

Application of the prevailing wage principle to pay rates of blue-collar federal employees dates from the 1860s. Wages for the 524,000 trade, craft and labor employees covered by the federal wage or blue-collar pay system are maintained in line with prevailing levels of pay for comparable work within each local wage area. Area wage surveys of the pay practices of private employers provide the data on which annual wage adjustments are based. In 1962, the principle of comparability was formally extended on a nationwide basis to white-collar federal employees. The general schedule, which applies to 1.4 million white-collar workers, is adjusted annually on the basis of a national survey of private employers representing a broad spectrum of occupations.[1] Increases in the rates for the uniformed services as well as several independent agencies are linked to the general schedule adjustments.

When job characteristics differ between public and private employment, assessing the comparability process is complicated. Since qualitative decisions must be made to determine work equivalency, the job matching process is inherently subjective. An extreme example of the difficulty is provided by the case of military personnel and law enforcement officers who have no direct counterparts in private employment. In the absence of an external standard for comparison, salaries must be approximated on the basis of private-sector rewards for a similar grouping of the skills required for these occupations.

State and local governments frequently resolve difficulties in determining the pay of police, fire fighters and sanitation workers by establishing a wage for one type of uniformed service worker and relating all others to this by way of an arbitrary ratio. For example, in New York City, fire fighters receive 100 percent of police officers' wages, and uniformed sanitation workers' rates are set at 90 percent of police pay. Unfortunately, wages which are, of necessity, subjectively derived may prove to be either higher or lower than the rate which would attract qualified workers to these jobs.

A number of studies have compared private- and public-sector pay rates. The Panel on Federal Compensation, established by President Ford in 1975, concluded that the principle of comparability had worked well for setting wage rates and that the practice should be continued.[2] On the other hand, a recent study by Sharon Smith of Princeton University which examines the relationship between comparable workers rather than comparable jobs concludes that federal employees were paid somewhat more than comparable private-sector workers.[3] However, Smith's underlying assumption that people of the same age with the same educational background and experience would follow the same career path has been criticized, and the study's conclusions are highly controversial.[4] Moreover, Smith found the greatest disparity in the pay of nonwhites, which may simply reflect significantly less dis-

---

1   The U.S. postal system is the only major federal pay system excluded from the strict comparison process. Since 1970, pay rates for 80 percent of the 864,000 postal service employees have been established through collective bargaining. However, the resulting agreements are subject to a requirement that total compensation (wages plus fringe benefits) be comparable to that available in the private sector for commensurate work.

2   *Staff Report of the President's Panel on Federal Compensation* (Washington, D.C., 1976), p.13.

3   Sharon P. Smith, *Equal Pay in the Public Sector: Fact or Fantasy* (Princeton: Princeton University, Industrial Relations Section, 1977), p. 20.

4   While age, education and experience certainly have an important effect on compensation, other factors also play a role. These factors include the classification of position or job rank held by the individual; the number of promotions and the rapidity of advancement in the organization; the nature of the industry and its profitability; the years of service within the organization and the accumulation of merit pay increases; the pay policies and management choices and influences in awarding pay to particular individuals.

crimination in the federal government.[5] At the state and local levels, Smith found that male workers actually received slightly less than equivalent private-sector males, while females received somewhat more. The higher pay for females may be due to less sex discrimination. On balance, therefore, it is generally accepted that wages of government workers are roughly comparable to pay in the private sector.

The question of whether public pay systems effectively meet government personnel objectives for attracting qualified employees at the least cost has received considerable attention. In addition to concern about pay rates, there is evidence that the exclusion of fringe benefits from the comparison of public and private compensation tends to understate government remuneration relative to private.

In response to this concern, the Panel on Federal Compensation recommended that leave benefits—such as paid vacation—and insurance benefits—such as health, disability and retirement pensions—should be included in comparing public and private compensation. A study is currently under way by the Department of Labor to devise the means for implementing this recommendation at the federal level.

RETIREMENT BENEFITS

Since retirement benefits represent 41 percent of fringe benefit expenditures, they constitute a major component of compensation for a comparison of total public and private remuneration. Unfortunately, neither public nor private plans show great uniformity in provisions, making precise direct comparison impossible. However, sectoral differences can be identified by contrasting the dominant government practice with that prevailing in industry.

Pension Benefits as Wage Replacement

Earnings from work represent the major source of income for most individuals. To alleviate the economic hardship of retirement, society has developed a complex wage replacement system. Social security, which is the major source of retirement income for most Americans, is the primary component of the income-maintenance network. Employer-sponsored pensions, where available, supplement this by providing additional benefits.[6]

The success of a pension in achieving its wage replacement goal is most frequently measured by its replacement rate. The total replacement rate is the ratio of social security and pension benefits to the worker's earnings before retirement. Certain guidelines exist for evaluating the adequacy of a replacement rate. At a minimum, benefits should replace enough income to meet the retiree's basic needs.

---

5   Since pensions are wage-related, discriminatory pay practices will be reflected in pension plan benefit awards. One would therefore expect to find that women and minorities receive less generous retirement incomes than similarly qualified white male workers. However, discrepancies in benefit awards should be far less pronounced for public than private pensions.

6   Public plans sponsored by excluded employers generally provide retirement benefits equivalent to social security plus a supplement.

Table 2–1. Retirement Income Equivalent to Preretirement Income for Married Couples Retiring January 1976, Selected Income Levels

Preretirement Income (dollars)	Preretirement Tax Payment (dollars)				Reduction in Expenses at Retirement[b] (dollars)	Equivalent Retirement Income[c]	
	Federal Income	OASDHI	State and Local Income[a]			Dollars	Percent of Preretirement Income
$ 4,000	$ 28	$234	$ 4		$ 544	$3,190	80
6,000	330	351	43		816	4,460	74
8,000	679	468	89		1,088	5,676	71
10,000	1,059	585	139		1,360	6,857	69
15,000	2,002	824	262		2,040	9,872	66

[a] In 1974, state and local income tax receipts were 13.1 percent of federal income tax receipts. This percentage probably rose in 1975 because federal taxes were decreased while state taxes increased. Therefore, the percentage of preretirement income needed to maintain living standards is probably slightly overstated.

[b] Consumption requirements for a two-person husband-wife family after retirement are 86.4 percent of those for a like family before retirement (aged 55 to 64). Savings are therefore estimated at 13.6 percent of preretirement income.

[c] Assumes that retirement income is not subject to tax. If retirement income is subject to taxation, a larger preretirement disposable income would be needed to yield the equivalent retirement income.

Sources: Commerce Clearing House, *1976 U.S. Master Tax Guide* (1975); Bureau of Labor Statistics, *Revised Equivalence Scale for Estimating Equivalent Incomes or Budget Costs by Family Type,* Bulletin 1570–2 (1968), p. 4; estimates of state and local income tax receipts as a percentage of federal income tax from Bureau of Economic Analysis.

At the other extreme, the maximum desirable replacement rate allows a worker to maintain preretirement consumption levels.

The preretirement consumption level is roughly equivalent to the final year's earnings net of taxes and savings.[7] However, when comparing pre- and postretirement consumption, expenses related to earning a living should also be subtracted from earnings since these expenditures are not incurred after retirement. Although medical expenses frequently increase upon retirement, Medicare benefits defray a portion of the cost. The net effect of reduced expenses and preferred tax treatment in retirement is that consumption levels equivalent to preretirement living standards can be maintained with replacement rates of 65 to 80 percent (see Table 2–1).

Cost-of-Living Adjustments. Even if replacement rates are established to maintain preretirement consumption levels, the retiree's living standard will decline over

---

7   Contributions to employer-sponsored plans as well as social security contributions by the employee are analogous to private savings efforts and therefore should be excluded from gross income when calculating consumption.

time as inflation erodes the purchasing power of benefits. Since the future pattern of cost-of-living increases cannot be predicted accurately, no amount of preplanning can ensure protection from inflation. The only way to insulate retirees from the erosion of their pension benefits is to provide cost-of-living adjustments which compensate for the full amount of price increases. In the absence of such adjustments, a retiree's economic welfare is entirely dependent upon the vagaries of the economy—a situation which undermines the establishment of a rational system of income maintenance.

Productivity Adjustments.   Automatic cost-of-living adjustments during retirement maintain workers' standards of living by preserving their command over goods and services. However, a retiree's economic position will decline relative to that of current workers because those still in the workforce receive increases for productivity improvements as well as inflation adjustments. Adjusting pension benefits in line with the growth in the average wage rather than tying increases to the consumer price index would permit retirees to share in productivity growth as well as protect them from price increases. Such an arrangement would prevent a deterioration in their position relative to employed workers.

The desirability of productivity increases is not as generally accepted as the need for inflation adjustments. Resistance centers on two points: the desirability of extending rewards for productivity gains to those who did not earn them and the ability of society to afford such increases. The philosophical debate over whether standards of living should be measured in real or relative terms is yet unsettled. However, the fact that social security ties postretirement increases to consumer price index movements will probably influence most employer-sponsored plans to limit adjustments to price increases.

Consideration of the appropriate lower and upper bounds in pension benefits as well as the desirability of some postretirement adjustments provide a useful benchmark against which to evaluate pension benefits in the public and private sectors.

The Level of Pension Benefits

The value of pension benefits depends on a variety of characteristics of pension plans. While the computation of the initial benefit and its relationship to previous earnings provides one measure of the level of benefits, the age at which benefits become available and the provision of postretirement inflation adjustments also figure importantly in any comparison.

A worker's total pension, however, depends crucially on whether the individual is also entitled to social security benefits. Therefore, in the following discussion it is important to remember that military personnel retiring after 1956 receive social security benefits in addition to their military retirement pay, while federal civil servants are not covered automatically by the social security program. At the state and local levels, the majority (85 percent) of general employees are covered, but only 36 percent of police and fire fighters are in plans covered by social security. All workers in the private sector are entitled to social security benefits.

Benefit Computation Formulas.   Defined benefit plans are the prevalent form of pension in both the public and private sectors. Civil service, military and 82 percent of state and local employees as well as 73 percent of those covered by private plans participate in pensions which relate benefits to salary and/or length of service by a predetermined formula.[8]

The most common benefit formulas in both sectors relate benefits to compensation as well as to length of service.[9] This type of benefit formula allocates benefit units, expressed as percentage points, for each year of creditable service. The product of these benefit units and years of service determines the percentage of the compensation base to which the employee is entitled at retirement. For example, an employee may earn 2 percent a year for 30 years and receive a pension benefit of 60 percent of the compensation base. Formulas, such as the preceding, which apply a uniform rate to each year of service are known as single-rate formulas and are the most prevalent kind in both private and civilian public plans.

An alternative type of unit benefit formula employs a system of rates which vary with length of service. The federal civil service is one of the largest systems using this technique. Civil servants accrue 1.5 percent for each of the first five years of service, 1.75 percent for each of the next five years, and 2 percent for each year thereafter, up to a maximum total accrual of 80 percent.[10] At the state-local levels, variable-rate formulas are most commonly employed in police and fire plans.

Although there is great diversity in the benefit formulas used by pension plans, it appears that public plan formulas are on average more liberal.[11] According to a Bankers Trust study, in the average corporate plan, a worker retiring after 30 years with $15,000 final salary would receive between 27 and 37 percent of the final-year's pay in addition to social security benefits.[12] If benefits were based on the final 3-

---

8   The figure for state-local employees covered by defined benefit plans from U.S. House of Representatives, Committee on Education and Labor, *Pension Task Force Report on Public Employee Retirement Systems*, 95th Cong., 2nd sess., March 15, 1978, Chapter B. Private employee figure based on unpublished raw data from the Department of Labor employee benefit security data base.

9   Flat benefit formulas which relate benefits only to compensation are sometimes found. Plans using this arrangement apply a fixed percentage to average wages regardless of years of employment. However, such formulas are only common among the federal uniformed services and local police and fire plans which require an extended period of service for pension eligibility and which mandate retirement within a few years of vestiture. Such plans typically provide replacement rates of 50 percent of final pay after 20 or 25 years of service. The military actually increases the replacement rate by 2.5 percentage points for each year of service. However, employees are not eligible for benefits unless they have at least 20 years of credit, and they may credit no more than 30 years to the pensions. Since retirements typically occur at the 20- or 30-year marks, this is effectively a dual flat benefit system providing 50 or 75 percent replacement.

10   ERISA requirements limit the spread in rates provided short-service and long-tenure employees under variable-rate private pensions. To ensure against backloading—i.e., unreasonably low benefit accruals for short service as compared to benefit accruals for long-service employees—rates applicable to later years of service may not exceed 133 ⅓ percent of the rate used for earlier service. Civil service just meets this stipulation as do most other public plans; however, according to the *Pension Task Force Report*, a small minority of public plans have backloaded formulas.

11   Public plans, on average, pay retired workers more; however, it must be noted that most public plans require employee contributions, while most private pensions are financed entirely by the employer.

12   *Bankers Trust Study of Corporate Pension Plans, 1975* (New York: Bankers Trust, 1975), p. 29.

Table 2-2. Average Annual Benefit Accrual and Benefits as a
Percent of High 3-Year Average Salary for Workers with
30 Years of Service Retiring from Public and Private
Plans, excluding Social Security

Item	Annual Benefit Accrual	Percent of Average Salary Replaced
Federal		
Civil service	1.87%	56
Military[a]	2.50	75
State and local		
Civilian	1.67	50
Police and fire[a,b]	2.50	50
Private	1.00	30

[a] Benefits are actually based on final pay rather than high-3 average salary. Annual benefit accruals and replacement rates would appear even more generous if translated to a high-3 bases.

[b] Police and fire plans consider 20 years to be a full career. Therefore, rates for these plans are based on 20 years of service.

Sources: *Bankers Trust Study of Corporate Pension Plans, 1975* (New York: Bankers Trust, 1975), pp. 29 and 96; Robert Tilove, *Public Employee Pension Funds* (New York: Columbia University Press, 1976), pp. 18-27; and U.S. House of Representatives, Committee on Education and Labor, *Pension Task Force Report on Public Employee Retirement Systems*, 95th Cong., 2nd sess., March 15, 1978, Chapter E.

years' average salary, this would be equivalent to an annual accrual rate of 1.12 percentage points. A new study, which includes the multiemployer as well as all the corporate plans, indicates that the average replacement rate in the private sector may be as low as 22 percent plus social security for male workers with 30 years of service.[13] Tilove estimates that the typical state-local plan provides an accrual rate of 1.67 percent when benefits are based on the final 3-years' average salary.[14] A worker with 30 years of service would therefore replace 50 percent of final average pay as well as being eligible for social security benefits. Federal pension programs have higher replacement rates. The federal civil service replaces 56 percent of a 30-year employee's high 3-year salary, but these workers are not covered by social security, while the military returns 75 percent of final basic pay with reduced social security benefits available at age 62 and full benefits at age 65. Table 2-2 shows replacement rates of typical public and private plans.

13   James H. Schulz, Leslie Kelly and Thomas Leavitt, "Private Pension Benefit Levels: Replacement Rates in 1975" (mimeo, 1978).

14   Robert Tilove, *Public Employee Pension Funds* (New York: Columbia University Press, 1976), p. 27.

Table 2–3. Comparison of Compensation Bases Used
in the Public and Private Sectors, 1975

Employer	Not Based on Actual Pay	1 Year or Less	2–4 Years	5 Years	Over 5 Years	Total
Federal	8.9%	24.4%	31.1%	35.6%	—	100%
Total state and local	21.9	27.6	17.6	27.7	5.5%	100
General employees	3.8	13.5	30.7	43.9	8.1	100
Police and fire	27.5	32.1	13.2	22.8	4.4	100
Teachers (including higher education)	—	5.2	48.9	36.7	9.2	100
Private	—	N.A.	0.8[a]	57.7	40.3	98.8[b]

[a] Includes 3-year terminal averages only.

[b] Figures add to 98.8 percent because 9.2 percent responses indicated a terminal average other than 3, 5 or 10 years. The unrecorded 1.2 percent may be greater or less than a 5-year average.

Sources: *Pension Task Force Report*, Table E-3, p. 114; and *Bankers Trust Study*, p. 27.

Compensation Base.   Not only are the accrual rates higher under public plans, but public plans also tend to use a shorter averaging period in calculating the compensation base.

Career averaging plans exist in both the public and private sectors; however, use of career-average salaries is more extensive among private plans. A survey of public plans revealed that 36 percent of federal plans and 33 percent of state and local systems employ an averaging period of five years or longer. In contrast, 38 percent of private plans use career averages, and an additional 60 percent employ terminal averages of five years or more. Even among plans using less than five years, public plans are more generous. Fifty-five percent of federal plans and 45 percent of state and local plans average less than five years of earnings, while only 1 to 2 percent of private plans employ such a short averaging period. Averaging periods of a year or less are rare among private plans; however, the federal uniformed services and a number of state-local police and fire plans employ the final day's pay as the basis for benefit calculation. A full 24 percent of federal plans and 28 percent of state and local systems employ a year or less as the averaging period (Table 2–3).

Final-average pay plans usually provide higher benefits since the inclusion of earlier years of earnings, which are usually lower than those of later years, depresses the base to which replacement percentages are applied.[15] The prevalence of shorter averaging periods among government pensions implies that compensation bases are more liberal in the public sector.

---

15   Final earnings plans would provide higher benefits as long as workers experience continually increasing earnings. Often, however, earnings profiles peak before retirement, in which case final earnings may more closely approximate career average. In an inflationary environment, nominal earnings probably increase each year, regardless of the individual's real earnings profile, so that final earnings plans generally yield higher benefits.

The federal uniformed services plan, despite the shorter averaging period, is a significant exception to the typically more generous compensation base in the public sector. Although some public plans relate benefits to compensation, including certain fringes, the majority of plans use salary alone as the compensation base. The federal uniformed services plan is based on salary alone, but, due to differences in the form of military and civilian compensation, the military base is actually smaller than that which would be used in a salary-only system for similarly compensated civilians. Regular military compensation (RMC) has four components: basic pay which is taxable cash income; basic allowance for quarters which varies by pay grade and dependency status; basic allowance for subsistence which is either a cash allowance or the value of meals provided; and the federal tax advantage which an individual accrues because the aforementioned cash allowances are not taxable. In addition, hazardous duty and incentive pays are not included in RMC. Since only basic pay is used for benefit calculation, the compensation base understates the participant's effective salary.[16] Military benefit formulas are therefore more generous than most other pension plans in order to offset the lower base used.

Integration with Social Security.   Some pension benefit formulas are designed to integrate with social security. Integration is intended to limit the employer's liability for pension benefits and to preclude employees from receiving excessively high replacement rates. Generally, the impact of integration is to offset the progressivity of the social security benefit formula because wage-related pension benefits for low-income workers do not exceed the cutoff or offset level by as much as those for high-income earners. Therefore, integrated plans tend to be less generous to low-wage workers.

Integrated benefit formulas are rare among public plans. Since civil service employees are excluded from social security coverage, social security benefits are not considered in the calculation of civil service pensions. The military system contains no integration provisions for service, age or disability benefits, and only 15 percent of state and local plans are integrated. In contrast, a 1974 study found that 60 percent of the 412,376 active corporate-type pension plans were integrated, which affected about 25 to 30 percent of the 30 million participants covered by private pensions.[17] The anomaly arises because small plans (with fewer than 26 participants) are more than twice as likely to be integrated with social security than are large plans.

Retirement Age.   The previous discussion has indicated that accrual rates under public plans are higher than for plans in the private sector, that the averaging period for public plans is generally shorter resulting in a higher compensation base, and that public plans are less likely to have integrated benefit formulas..This tendency for benefits to be more generous in the public sector is reinforced by the fact that

---

16   The components of compensation mentioned here are akin to salary rather than fringes such as leaves.

17   Raymond Schmitt, "Integration of Private Pension Plans with Social Security," *Studies in Public Welfare*, paper 18, prepared for the Subcommittee on Fiscal Policy of the Joint Economic Committee, 93rd Cong., 2nd sess., 1974.

many public employees are eligible for benefits at an earlier retirement age. Although 65 is the normal retirement age in the vast majority of private plans,[18] 60 to 62 are the ages used for public pensions covering civilian employees.[19] Normal retirement ages for police and fire employees are generally lower: ages 50 to 55 with 20 years' service are typical. Federal military personnel as well as many state and local uniformed employees need only meet a length-of-service requirement of 20 years in order to draw full benefits.[20]

Optional retirement ages are a common feature among public plans covering civilian employees. Full benefits frequently are available at earlier ages to employees with long service records. Typically, the alternative ages are 50 or 55 with 30 years of service. For example, the federal civil service plan offers three optional retirement schemes: age 55 with 30 years of service; age 60 with 20 years of service; or age 62 with 5 years of service.

The retirement age at which the worker is eligible for full benefits is higher under most private plans; however, early retirement provisions which allow employees to draw reduced benefits at a younger age are more common in the private than public sector. Uniformed service plans (police, fire and military) have no such provisions, while the civil service retirement system provides benefits for long-term (20 to 25 years) employees who have been involuntarily separated through no fault of their own. Generally, the only plans that provide for early retirement are state plans for general employees and large state-administered plans for teachers.[21] In contrast, 90 percent of the private plans surveyed by Bankers Trust permitted employees to elect early retirement.[22]

Reduction of benefits upon election of early retirement can take on one of two forms. The prevailing practice among public plans is actuarial reduction whereby the annual benefit is reduced by an amount which roughly offsets the longer period of time over which payments must be made. This can take the form of a reduction of 6 or 7 percent for each year that the retiring employee is younger than the normal retirement age. The alternative, which is the dominant practice in industry, is to provide a benefit which is greater than the actuarial equivalent though somewhat less than the full benefit. Almost 80 percent of the plans in the Bankers Trust survey reduced benefits by less than the full actuarial deduction at early retirement, and 8 percent provided the full accrued benefit.

---

18   The growing importance of collectively bargained plans which permit retirement after 30 years of service may have reduced the average retirement age in the private sector somewhat.

19   Ninety-five percent of the plans studied by Bankers Trust cite 65 as the normal retirement age (*Bankers Trust Study*, pp. 24, 25.) In contrast, federal civil servants may retire at age 62 with 5 years of service; teachers in large state systems may retire at age 60 with 10 years of service; general state employees often retire at age 60 with 5 or 10 years of service; and municipal systems frequently allow age 62 with 5 or 10 years of service.

20   *Pension Task Force Report*, Table E–1.

21   Ibid., Chapter E.

22   *Bankers Trust Study*, pp. 10–15.

Overall, it appears that employees may retire at roughly the same ages in the public and private sectors. However, public employees retiring at early ages under optional retirement schemes receive more generous benefits than private employees retiring with actuarially reduced benefits.

Employee Contributions

When differences in benefit formulas, averaging periods and retirement age are examined, public pensions appear considerably more generous than private pensions. However, when employee contributions are taken into consideration, the differential between private and public benefits narrows substantially.

The tax advantages available for employer contributions to private pension plans have created a strong incentive for qualified plans to finance benefits exclusively through employer contributions. Private plans are predominantly noncontributory— none of the Bankers Trust study plans required employee contributions. In contrast, public plans normally require employee contributions of 5 to 7 percent of wages. The effect of the contributions on the differential in benefit plans is apparent in a survey by the New York State Department of Labor. A worker retiring at age 65 with 30 years of service received 49 percent of the final $10,000 salary if covered by a public plan compared to 24 percent for a worker in private employment. Once the public-employee pension is calculated net of the employee contributions, the replacement rate drops to 34 percent—a figure substantially closer to the 24 percent for a private pension. For workers with shorter service or lower income, the difference is almost completely eliminated by adjusting for employee contributions (see Table 2–4).

Cost-of-Living Adjustments.   Up to this point, the discussion of relative benefit levels has been focused entirely on the initial replacement rate. However, even if private benefits were initially equivalent in generosity to public payments, they would most likely decline in relative status over time due to the impact of inflation.

Public employees are far more likely to receive at least a limited guarantee of protection from inflation-induced erosion of pension benefits. Although private employers occasionally may provide ad hoc postretirement benefit increases, only 6 percent of industry plans adjust benefits in accordance with the consumer price index.[23] In contrast, federal employees and 50 percent of participants in state and local plans are protected by automatic adjustment mechanisms.[24] Federal provisions tend to be more generous than those of lower-level governmental units. The federal government guarantees the full value of consumer price index increases, while state-local plans typically limit adjustments to 3 percent per year. The rare private plan which offers automatic adjustment is likely to have a similar cap on increases.

In time of rapid inflation such as that experienced during 1973–74, the absence

---

23   Ibid., p. 30.

24   Almost all of the remaining state and local workers receive periodic ad hoc adjustments to benefits. However, it must be noted that most government employees do not work 30 years and earn these benefits. In fact, according to the *Pension Task Force Report*, only one-third of government employees earn their full vested rights.

Table 2–4. Comparison of Pension Benefits of General Employees and Teachers, State and Local Government with Those of Employees Covered by Pension Plans in Private Industry, New York State, as of January 1, 1972

Employee			Median Pension as Percent of Final Salary				Public Employee Pensions, Net of Value of Employee Contributions
			Exclusive of Primary Social Security		Inclusive of Primary Social Security		
Age	Service	Final Salary	Public Employees	Private Employees	Public Employees	Private Employees	
65	20	$ 5,000	32.1	22	66.2	62.1	22.4
		10,000	32.4	17	53.7	42.9	22.7
		14,000	32.4	17	46.3	35.5	22.7
	30	5,000	48.1	29	80.0	69.1	33.7
		10,000	48.6	24	67.6	49.9	34.1
		14,000	48.6	22	66.2	40.5	34.1
60*	20	5,000	30.5	19	61.7	60.9	20.3
		10,000	31.7	14	51.9	42.3	22.2
		14,000	32.1	13	45.0	33.3	22.4
	30	5,000	47.2	28	77.3	69.9	32.0
		10,000	48.1	22	64.9	50.3	35.6
		14,000	48.1	20	59.9	40.3	35.6

*Benefits shown only for plans paying benefits at the indicated age; the fact that some plans do not pay benefits at these ages is not reflected in the medians.

Source: Tilove, *Public Employee Pension Funds*, pp. 58–59.

of cost-of-living adjustments to benefits imposes a significant hardship on retirees. For this reason, pension plans—both public and private—have faced mounting pressure to provide inflation adjustments. The 1972 Amendments to the Social Security Act introduced automatic cost-of-living adjustments for social security benefits. Unlike governmental units which may rely on general revenues to finance inflation adjustments, private employers who are constrained by profitability requirements are resistant to diverting operating revenues for this purpose. Moreover, since future inflation rates cannot be predicted accurately, private plans are not always able to profund adequately future adjustments even if such a strategy were considered desirable. For these reasons, it is not likely that automatic inflation adjustments will become prevalent in industry plans. When lifetime benefits are considered, this sectoral difference may be the most important determinant of a benefit differential favoring public employees.

Summary

Primarily because of the availability of postretirement cost-of-living adjustments, pension benefits for affected public employees are definitely higher than those provided for employees in the private sector. Earlier retirement ages in the public sector also increase the lifetime value of benefits. Furthermore, only half the wage earners and salaried employees in the private sector are covered under private employer-financed retirement plans, while almost the entire public employee population is covered under a public plan.

On the other hand, the level of benefits for most public employees is not excessive, especially considering that public employees contribute to their pensions while private-sector employees do not. Replacement rates generally do not exceed those required to maintain previous living standards, and the cost-of-living adjustment is a rational method of protecting workers from unexpected erosion of their retirement income. However, in those instances when public employees are also entitled to social security, the combined benefits replace an excessively high level of preretirement income. Furthermore, in those plans not covered by social security, workers can achieve insured status under social security and earn additional benefits which, when added to their regular public benefit, results in excessive rates of replacement. However, both these anomalies result from the lack of coordination between social security and public plans and not from excessive public benefit levels.

DISABILITY BENEFITS

The social security disability program is the major source of income for severely disabled Americans. However, not all disabled workers are eligible for social security benefits. In contrast to the civil service, military and some state-local plans, social security defines disability rather narrowly. Social Security Disability Insurance requires that "an individual must have a disability so severe that he is unable to engage in any substantial gainful activity; the impairment must be a medically determinable physical or mental condition that is expected to continue for at least 12 months or result in death.''[25] An impairment which renders the worker incapable of doing only a specific job, therefore, does not qualify the employee for benefits. Other workers, such as federal civil service employees and some state and local workers, are naturally excluded since their employers do not participate in the social security program.

Public- and private-sector practices on providing for disability differ markedly. On balance, the net effect of these differences is that public-sector benefits are more generous.

Determination of Disability.   The definition of disability varies widely among different plans; however, most definitions will fall in one of three major categories: (1) total and permanent disability, as defined under social security, which prevents the individual from engaging in any substantial gainful employment for at least 12 months; (2) total disability which renders the individual incapable of performing any job within a specific organization; and (3) partial disability which makes an individual incapable of performing some essential part of a specific job.

The federal civil service program incorporates a relatively lenient definition of disability. An employee is eligible for benefits if the worker has ''a physical or mental condition which prevents him from satisfactorily performing some of any essential part of the duties of the position to which he is officially assigned, or which prevents him from functioning on the total job without hazard to himself or others.''[26] No differentiation is made between degrees of disability so that partially and totally disabled workers are eligible for the same benefits. Even if it is within their physical and mental capabilities, partially disabled employees are not required to accept another position.

Establishing the existence of a disability begins with an application by the employee or employing agency accompanied by a statement from the individual's supervisor showing how the worker's condition affects job performance. This must be supported by a report from the employee's doctor fully describing the disability. To verify the validity of the claim and establish whether the impairment is temporary or permanent, the Civil Service Commission may also require an additional medical examination by an approved physician. Despite the existence of numerous cross checks, the definition is quite lenient as 95 percent of disability applications are approved.[27]

Discontinuance of disability benefits can result from either medical recovery or reestablishment of earning power. For those retired under the temporary disability provisions, physical examinations may be required annually until the retiree reaches age 60 or is reclassified as permanently disabled. Regardless of the persistence of a temporary or permanent impairment, restoration of earnings will cause the termination of disability payments. However, the earnings test is very liberal since the retiree can earn up to 80 percent of the current rate of pay in a preretirement job

---

25   Robert J. Myers, *Summary of the Provisions of the OASDHI, and the Supplementary Medical Insurance System* (Philadelphia: Temple University, 1977).

26   *Federal Employee Retirement Systems* (New York: Tax Foundation, Inc., 1978), p. 26, 27.

27   Report of the Comptroller General of the United States, *Civil Service Disability Retirement: Needed Improvements* (Washington, D.C., 1976), p. 12.

for two consecutive years before benefits will be terminated. This qualification can be easily abused by persons with the flexibility to adjust their income or hours worked because high earnings in one year can be offset by earnings below the 80 percent level in the next year. Moreover, the absence of systematic verification of the accuracy of reported data hampers enforcement of the earnings requirement. Obviously, neither the medical nor earnings tests are very stringent since less than 1 percent of persons classified as disabled are removed from the rolls because of medical recovery or excess earned income.[28]

Civil service disability payments totaled $1.6 billion in 1976. Beneficiaries numbered 279,000 or 20 percent of total civil service annuitants.[29] Furthermore, the number of disabilities per 100,000 covered employees has increased dramatically from 724 in 1960 to 1,128 in 1974.[30] The high incidence of disability among federal civil servants reflects the lenient eligibility criteria and liberal implementation of the program.

The Department of Defense generally conforms with Civil Service Commission guidelines for benefit eligibility, except that the military distinguishes different degrees of disability. Persons who have less than 20 years of service must be at least 30 percent disabled to be eligible for an annuity. Members rated less than 30 percent disabled who have completed more than 20 years of service are eligible for full benefits, while those with less than 20 years of service are eligible for a lump-sum separation payment.

Disability retirees may choose to receive an annuity either from the Department of Defense, the Veteran's Administration or a combination of the two. Many retirees elect to receive their disability annuity from the VA since differences in the definition of disability and the tax status of benefits frequently make VA annuities more generous than those provided by the uniformed services plan. Unlike the military, the VA will provide benefits for permanent disabilities rated as low as 10 percent.[31] Moreover, the VA considers only whether the disability will impair earning potential for any job in the economy, while DOD focuses solely on the disabled's ability to perform military duties. As a result, the VA may rate individuals as more severely disabled than the armed forces does. The differences in the two organizations' definitions of disability require dual examinations, ratings and adjudications of each case.

 Two other features of VA benefits frequently make them more attractive than DOD annuities. Unlike the uniformed services plan which relates benefits to level of basic pay, the VA provides flat dollar amounts which vary only with the degree

---

28   Ibid., p. 19.

29   Social Security Administration, Office of Research and Statistics, "Benefits and Beneficiaries under Public Employee Retirement Systems, Calendar Year, 1976," Research and Statistics Note #8 (Washington, D.C., July 1978), Table 1, p. 4.

30   Raymond L. Eck and Edwin C. Hustead, "Disability Experience Under the Civil Service Retirement System—1955 to 1974," *Journal of Occupational Medicine*, Vol. 18 (January 1976), pp. 45–50.

31   The VA ratings do not take into account years of service.

of disability. For individuals of low rank who have low earnings, the flat dollar award may be greater than a wage-related annuity from the Department of Defense. Second, VA benefits are completely tax-exempt, whereas DOD annuities are only partially tax-exempt.[32] For this reason, even individuals who are entitled to a higher benefit from the uniformed services plan will opt for taking a portion of their benefit from the VA if the VA award exceeds the cutoff point for tax exemption on the military benefit. Because there is a 100 percent offset integrating VA and military benefits, a retiree receiving a combination benefit is not doubly compensated, although the individual does get the full amount of the highest possible award. However, as in the case of regular military benefits, VA pensions are not integrated with social security.

Members of the uniformed services are eligible to receive further help from the VA. In addition to benefits for nonservice-connected disabilities, services are available from the following agencies: the VA Vocational Rehabilitation Service, Veteran's Administration Alcohol and Drug Dependency Service, Specially Adapted Housing for Disabled Vets Program, Specially Adapted Autos for Disabled Vets Program, and the U.S. Soldier's and Airmen's Home.

As in the case of civil service, qualification and administration are lenient. The Defense Audit Service estimates that 25 percent of those classified as disabled because they could not perform a specific job could have been productively employed in other positions.[33] On the other hand, the armed forces believes retirement to be more efficient than reemployment; because most of these disabled employees are enlisted personnel, the high cost of retraining them usually could not be recouped before the end of the worker's "hitch."

Perhaps the best indicator of the military's lenient qualification and administration is the high incidence of disability retirees. As of 1976, 51 percent of veteran and military annuitants had retired on disability in contrast to 17 percent for the government as a whole.[34] Furthermore, the incidence of disability has increased

---

32   Disability benefits from the uniformed services plan are equal to the higher of either 2.5 percent of basic pay times years of service or percent of disability times basic pay. The federal tax exemption only applies to the amount which would be produced by the latter calculation even if the actual award is higher due to calculations based on the first method. For example, an employee with 30 percent disability and 20 years of service would receive a benefit of 50 percent of basic pay according to the first method but only 30 percent of basic pay calculated the second way. The benefit he or she receives will be the higher one, 50 percent. However, only that portion of his or her benefit equal to 30 percent of pay is tax-exempt. The Tax Reform and Simplification Act of 1976 further tightened the tax exemption by restricting it to disability benefits awarded for injuries incurred in actual or simulated combat for employees who entered after September 25, 1976.

33   Defense Audit Service, *Report on the Audit of the Department of Defense Civilian Disability Retirements*, Report #858 (Washington, D.C., February 1978).

34   This is based on Table 1–2 in Chapter 1. The figure for percent of military annuitants retired on disability is calculated including veterans programs since this is the major source of retirement income for disabled military. However, because individuals may draw benefits from both programs, the figure is slightly overstated due to double counting. The figure for all federal excludes veterans programs to avoid biasing results since the number of beneficiaries of VA programs is more than double that of all other federal systems.

Table 2-5. State and Local Retirees, Survivors and Terminated Vested Employees

System Category	Percent of Inactive Members			
	Retired on Age or Service	Retired on Disability	Survivor Beneficiaries	Terminated with Vested Benefits
Total state and local	73.9	6.5	8.8	10.8
General government workers	74.4	6.9	9.0	9.7
Police and fire fighters	56.4	17.3	25.0	1.3
Teachers	76.7	3.5	5.0	14.8

Source: *Pension Task Force Report*, Table 15, p. 216.

dramatically from 37 per 1,000 employees in 1965 to 78 per 1,000 in 1975.[35]

Although definitions of disability vary widely among state and local systems, the typical plan requires the employee to be totally and permanently disabled in order to receive benefits. The incidence of disability retirees appears to be considerably lower at the state-local levels than at the federal level (see Table 2-5). As expected, a larger percentage of fire fighters and police retire with disability pensions.

About 80 percent of the country's largest private employers provide plans with disability retirement provisions. Although definitions of disability vary, most plans provide benefits for a "total disability" when the employee is physically or mentally incapable of productively working for the company. Whether this is limited to a specific job or to any job within the company depends on the specific disability policy.

Although plans in both the public and private sectors are typically less rigorous than social security, disability definitions are generally even more lenient in public than private employment. Civil service, military and a number of state and local plans provide benefits for partial disability. In contrast, the vast majority of industry plans require total incapacitation. Naturally, this more rigorous definition lowers the incidence and the cost of disability for the employer.

Length-of-Service Requirements. Another way in which private plans limit their liabilities for disability is through stringent length-of-service requirements. Ten to 15 years is the typical minimum qualification period in private plans, while public plans generally require only 5 to 10 years of service.[36] Civil service employees, for example, are eligible for benefits after only 5 years of creditable service. The uniformed services also fall in the 5- to 10-year range requiring 8 years to qualify for disability pensions.[37]

---

35   *Federal Employee Retirement Systems*, p. 27.

36   *Bankers Trust Study*, pp. 15–16.

37   Under the military plan, if the employee's disability is a result of active service, there is no length of service requirement.

Level of Disability Benefits.   Disability benefits, like retirement benefits, are usually based on length of service as well as level of compensation.

Under civil service, disability beneficiaries are guaranteed a minimum of 40 percent of the average of their three years of highest pay. Amounts above the minimum are calculated on the basis of the variable-rate unit benefit formula used for retirement.

For military personnel, the amount of the annuity is calculated by multiplying the member's basic pay with either percent of disability or 2.5 percent for each year of service. In either case, the disability benefit cannot exceed 75 percent of basic pay.

At the state and local levels, police and fire plans generally provide benefits around 50 percent of salary for ordinary disability. However, one-third of the systems have special provisions which relax service requirements and increase benefits for service-connected disability. For example, police and fire plans pay from two-thirds to three-fourths of pay for duty disability.[38]

For general state and local workers, regular benefits can be quite low for young employees since replacement rates are typically based on length of service. However, minimum benefit provisions often establish a floor of 25 to 33 percent of average salary under disability benefit levels.

·   A comparison of public disability benefits with those provided in the private sector is very difficult since private employees usually have access to a variety of sources of disability income. A single company may make disability benefits available from any one or more of the following sources: salary continuance, accident and sickness insurance, long-term disability insurance (LTD), group life insurance, pension plan, thrift plan, and profit-sharing plan. LTD usually involves minimal length-of-service requirements which enhance the protection for short-service employees. LTD can bring replacement rates up to the 40 to 60 percent range enjoyed in the public sector, plus social security.[39]

Normal Retirement Age.   When a disability retiree reaches normal retirement age, both public (except civil service) and private plans increase benefits. The disability retiree is shifted to normal retirement status and receives a replacement rate equivalent to the rate that would have been received had the retiree continued working to normal retirement age.

In some cases, the switch to normal retirement status involves a change in the tax treatment of benefits. Up to 1978, the first $100 of weekly disability benefits was tax-exempt until the worker reached normal retirement age. As a result of 1976 legislation, the favorable tax provision has been narrowed to apply only to persons who meet the social security qualifications of total and permanent disability.[40] How-

---

38   Tilove, *Public Employee Pension Funds.*

39   *Death and Disability Benefits for Salaried Employees of the 50 Largest U.S. Industrial Companies as of July 1, 1974* (Washington, D.C.: Wyatt Company, 1975), p. 6. Due to the fact that only large companies are represented in this sample, replacement rates provided by group insurance arranged through these employers may be more liberal than those provided by insurance policies contracted by private companies in general.

40   Tax Reform and Simplification Act, 94th Cong., 2nd sess. (enacted October 1976). According to provisions of the law, the individual must also be retired and under age 65.

ever, when those eligible for the $100 exemption reach the normal retirement age, their benefits are taxed in the same way as old-age retirement benefits.

Cost-of-Living Adjustments.   The same pattern of cost-of-living adjustments applies to disability benefits as to retirement benefits. The federal programs provide full adjustments for inflation; some state and local plans also adjust for increases in prices but usually with a cap; and private plans generally do not include cost-of-living adjustments.

PROTECTION FOR SURVIVORS

Survivor benefits are considerably more generous for federal pension plans than for those at the state-local levels and for private plans. For both the civil service and military, preretirement death benefits are available. For death after retirement, survivor options are provided at less than a full actuarial reduction in the employee pension. All federal benefits are adjusted for increases in the consumer price index. Some state and local plans provide preretirement death benefits, but survivor protection after retirement is usually purchased by the retiree through an actuarially reduced pension. For private pensions, some supplementary preretirement benefits are provided, but, as in the case of state and local plans, many employees must purchase postretirement protection through joint and survivor options. Neither the private plans nor the state and local plans provide full cost-of-living adjustments.

In private plans, protection for survivors has become increasingly widespread. Preretirement death benefits for a spouse were provided by 63 percent of all plans surveyed in the 1975 Bankers Trust study compared to 28 percent of plans in the 1965 study.[41] Preretirement death benefits are designed to supplement the group life insurance that most companies provide. These benefits fill the gap in pension plans for the employee who dies within 10 or 15 years of normal retirement age after accruing a substantial benefit. In the case of death after retirement, ERISA encourages the trend toward awarding a portion of a deceased employee's accrued benefits to his or her spouse. As of 1976, all private plans have had to include at least a 50 percent joint and survivor annuity option which will automatically become effective upon retirement unless the pensioner chooses otherwise.

Under civil service, survivor benefits are more generous. Survivor pensions are payable to widows, widowers and dependent children of deceased active workers. Although no age requirement exists for widow and widower benefits, benefits are discontinued in the case of remarriage before age 60. In the case of death after retirement, widow and widower pensions are available unless the employee pensioner elects not to take a reduction in that pension. However, the reduction is quite minimal and does not reflect the full actuarial cost of providing the additional protection. The maximum amount of the widow or widower pension is 55 percent of the unreduced pension for which the retired member was eligible.

Survivor benefits under the military retirement system are parallel to those under civil service. Retirees may elect a survivorship option which provides a post-

---

41   *Bankers Trust Study,* p. 18.

retirement death annuity equal to 55 percent of the retired pay. However, unlike civil service, military survivor benefits are integrated with social security. The military survivor benefit is reduced by the portion of the spouse's OASDHI benefit which is attributable solely to military coverage under OASDHI. Both the civil service and military survivor benefits are subject to automatic adjustments twice annually for changes accumulated in the cost of living.

At the state and local levels, about half of the systems provide lump-sum death benefits to survivors of workers killed in active service. This can take the form of either a refund of employee contributions with interest or a lump-sum survivors payment if greater. The other half of state-local plans provides annuities for widows and children of members who die in active service. Such provisions are typical of plans not covered by social security. Those systems with social security coverage often rely on social security for protection of dependent survivors, although 57.7 percent have some form of survivor annuities in addition.[42] Generally, this additional protection is found in municipal plans which were organized before social security coverage was expanded. Police and fire plans provide annuities ranging from 25 to 50 percent of pay if death is not service-connected and up to two-thirds of final pay if death is duty-connected. As expected, plans without social security have low length-of-service requirements, generally 5 years or less, while eligibility in systems with social security tends to be longer, generally 10 years or more.

Provision for survivors in the case of death after retirement must usually be purchased by the employee. Retired workers can elect a joint and survivor option whereby the employee's own pension, payable during lifetime, is reduced actuarially to pay for the survivor's protection. Alternatives include a modified cash refund or a return of reserve. With a modified cash refund plan, if the benefits paid to a pensioner through a straight-life annuity do not equal the amount of the retiree's contribution account at retirement, the balance is paid to the survivor. Under the return-of-reserve scheme, the value of the entire pension is determined at retirement, and if pension benefits do not exceed this amount, the balance is paid to the retiree's beneficiary.

SUMMARY

The preceding analysis shows that total compensation tends to be higher in the public than private sector. Although average wages for government and private employees are about equal, public pension benefits are more generous.

The value of retirement benefits depends on three components: the initial benefit; the length of the period over which benefits are received; and the availability of cost-of-living adjustments. At first glance, it appears that public plans generally offer higher initial benefits than private plans. However, unlike private workers, many public employees, such as civil service workers as well as almost all state-local employees, contribute to their pensions, and these contributions partially, if not

---

42 *Pension Task Force Report*, Table 32, p. 247.

fully, offset the differential in initial benefit levels. Some policy makers have suggested that, in order to avoid public misconception, public plans be restructured in order to establish a clear distinction between benefits which are due to employee contributions and those financed by employer contributions.[43]

The other two characteristics of many public retirement plans make benefits significantly more generous than those provided by private plans. Public employees are often eligible for retirement at a younger age—60 to 62 for general state employees and 50 to 55 for uniformed state workers and federal employees. In contrast private employees who retire before 65 usually receive reduced retirement payments. In addition to earlier retirement ages, federal pensions and some state and local pensions provide at least partial cost-of-living adjustments whereas very few private plans offer similar protection.

Other pension provisions such as disability and survivor protection are sometimes superior under public plans. The definition of disability, the length-of-service required and especially at the federal level, and lenient administration make public pension plans more generous than private. Survivor protection, especially for federal employees, is better in public than private pension plans.

In summary, while wages and perhaps the initial retirement benefits paid in relation to previous earnings are about equal in the public and private sectors, other aspects of the public pension plans are more generous than private pension plans. These differences are greatest for federal employees and for uniformed workers at the state-local levels.

---

43   This differentiation between employer- and employee-financed benefits may not be justified, however, as economic theory suggests that employees generally pay through lower wages for employer pension contributions.

3

Financing Public Pensions

Retirement benefit costs have grown dramatically at all levels of government, and public pensions are likely to become even more expensive as increasing numbers of public employees retire. The current and future costs of the public-employee pension plans have significant implications for both the retirement security of government workers and the tax liability of the general public. This chapter first examines current costs of the various public retirement systems and the sources of their financing. The second section discusses the impact of employment patterns, demographic changes and economic variables on future costs. The final section explores the current funding status of public plans and evaluates the advantages and potentiality of fully funded plans in the public sector.

CURRENT COSTS AND FINANCING

In 1976, state-local systems, federal civil service and the military each dispensed about $8 billion, or a total of $24 billion, in benefits to approximately 4 million beneficiaries (see Table 3–1). These figures compare to $75 billion in benefits and 33 million beneficiaries under social security and $15 billion and 7 million beneficiaries from private plans in 1975.[1] The increase in benefits and beneficiaries is summarized in Table 3–2. Total benefits for each system increased at least sevenfold between 1960 and 1976, while the number of military beneficiaries was more than four times the 1960 level. Even in constant dollars, the total benefits increased more than fourfold over the 1960–76 period. This rapid growth primarily reflects substantial increases in employment and in the number of employees retiring.

In addition to the rapid growth in benefits, $166.2 billion of assets are currently held by government pensions to support some portion of future benefits promised to current retirees and workers. Table 3–3 presents the growth of asset holdings of all public and private pension plans including social security. The $117.3 billion of reserves held by state and local pension funds in 1976 amounts to more than 40 percent of the total funds held by all private-sector plans.

Employee and Employer Contributions

Benefits and asset accumulation in public plans are supported by contributions from employees and expenditures by the employing government agency. Although

---

1   Martha Remy Yohalem, "Employee Benefit Plans, 1975," *Social Security Bulletin*, Vol. 40, No. 11 (November 1977), Table 3, p. 23.

Table 3-1. **Benefits and Beneficiaries under Public-Employee Retirement Systems, 1976**

Retirement System	Total Benefit Payments (millions)	Beneficiaries as of June 30 (thousands)
State and local systems	$7,700.0	1,840.0
Federal contributory systems	8,681.2	1,441.8
Federal civil service	8,584.4	1,432.0
Foreign service	71.2	4.6
Tennessee Valley Authority	21.7	4.7
Federal Reserve Board	2.6	0.3
Federal judiciary survivors	1.3	0.2
Federal noncontributory systems	7,864.5	1,158.6
Military	7,673.7	1,131.8
Coast Guard	129.4	17.6
Federal Reserve Banks	25.5	6.9
Public health service	26.0	1.6
Federal judiciary	7.0	0.2
Environmental science services	2.3	0.1
Canal Zone construction	0.2	0.4
Tax court	0.4	*

* Less than 500,000.

Source: Social Security Administration, Office of Research and Statistics, "Benefits and Beneficiaries under Public Employee Retirement Systems, Calendar Year, 1976," Research and Statistics Note #8 (Washington, D.C., July 11, 1978).

most of these payments are employer financed, employee contributions represent a significant portion of total revenues. According to estimates for fiscal 1975, 35 percent of contributions to state and local plans were made by employees and 16 percent of federal contributions were worker financed. These high percentages contrast sharply with less than 8 percent contributions by employees to private plans and reflect the higher incidence of contributory plans in the public sector. Virtually all federal civilian employees and 85 percent of state and local workers are required to help finance pension costs.[2] Contribution rates for employees are generally between 5 and 7 percent of total earnings. The most common rate for locally administered plans is 5 percent; for state administered plans the typical rate is 6 percent, and for almost all federal plans the required contribution is 7 percent. Members of the federal uniformed services, representing about 45 percent of the federal workforce, are the only major group of public employees that participate in a noncontributory plan.

2   U.S. House of Representatives, Committee on Education and Labor, *Pension Task Force Report on Public Employee Retirement Systems*, 95th Cong., 2nd sess., March 15, 1978, p. 135.

Table 3–2.   Benefits and Beneficiaries of Public Pension Plans, 1940–76, Selected Years

	State-Local		Civil Service		Military*	
Year	Benefits (millions)	Beneficiaries (thousands)	Benefits (millions)	Beneficiaries (thousands)	Benefits (millions)	Beneficiaries (thousands)
1940	$ 125	152	$ 68	63	$ 52	32
1945	173	208	94	86	74	37
1950	320	294	192	172	290	125
1955	595	427	379	296	471	187
1960	1,021	660	816	575	751	264
1965	1,775	886	1,385	728	1,505	485
1970	3,280	1,291	2,819	959	3,133	773
1976	7,700	1,840	8,563	1,432	7,674	1,132

*Data for the military were estimated on the basis of the 1974 and 1975 ratio of military to "other federal employees."

Sources: Social Security Administration, *Social Security Bulletin,* Annual Statistical Supplement, 1975; and Research and Statistics Note #8.

Table 3–3.   Asset Holdings of Private and Public Pension Funds, Book Value, End of Year, 1940–76, Selected Years (billions of dollars)

	Year							
Retirement System	1940	1945	1950	1955	1960	1965	1970	1976
Private pensions	$2.0	$5.4	$12.1	$27.5	$52.0	$86.5	$138.2	$279.6
Insured	0.6	2.6	5.6	11.3	18.8	27.3	41.2	98.1
Noninsured	1.4	2.8	6.5	16.1	33.1	59.2	97.0	181.5
Public pensions	2.0	7.1	13.7	21.7	20.3	18.2	32.5	35.4
OASDI	1.6	2.5	5.3	10.5	19.3	33.1	58.2	117.3
State-local	0.6	2.3	4.2	6.6	10.6	15.9	23.1	45.8
Federal civilian	0.1	0.7	2.6	3.5	3.7	3.9	4.4	3.1
Railroad retirement	—	—	—	—	—	—	—	—
Military								

Source: Figures taken from annual surveys by the Securities and Exchange Commission published in the SEC's *Statistical Bulletin,* Vol. 37, No. 5 (May 1978), p. 8.

Table 3-4.   Ratio of Beneficiaries to Employment in Public Plans, 1950-75, Selected Years

Year	Civil Service	Military	State and Local
1950	.081	.095	.068
1955	.125	.059	.084
1960	.213	.098	.103
1965	.282	.175	.111
1970	.333	.246	.127
1975	.475	.496	.143

Source: Adapted from Alicia H. Munnell and Ann M. Connolly, "Funding Government Pensions: State-Local, Civil Service and Military," in *Funding Pensions: Issues and Implications for Financial Markets*, Conference Series No. 16 (Federal Reserve Bank of Boston, October 1976).

The predominance of contributory plans in the public sector is difficult to understand since all participants in public plans are eligible for the same tax benefits available to members of qualified private plans. Under the current law, employer contributions to a pension plan are not considered part of the worker's income until that worker begins to receive benefits. By deferring the tax on employer contributions until retirement, the worker receives the equivalent of an interest-free loan from Treasury. Also, since income typically declines in retirement and special tax provisions for the elderly further lower the marginal tax rate faced by the retired beneficiary, that person will probably end up paying less tax than that paid while working.

These tax considerations may provide a partial explanation for the growing trend toward elimination of mandatory employee-contribution requirements to public plans. Contributions for at least some employees have now been eliminated in over 30 percent of state-local plans so that nearly 15 percent of state-local employees no longer contribute to their plans.[3]

Combined Contribution Rates

The magnitude of the combined employee-employer contribution varies considerably from plan to plan. Contributions, as a percent of payroll, average 16 percent for large state and local plans, 18 percent for smaller state-local systems, 26 percent for the federal civil service, and 40 percent for the military system. These contribution rates are highly correlated with the benefit payout rate (benefits as a percent of payrolls) for each of the systems. For large state and local plans, the payout rate

---

3   Ibid.

averages 7.9 percent of payroll, while the federal civil service payout rate exceeds 20 percent, and the military plan has a rate of 40 percent.[4]

The variation in payout rates primarily reflects differences in the relative "maturity" of systems rather than the level of average pension benefits. Newly established plans tend to have a very low ratio of beneficiaries to active participants since only a small percentage of the newly covered workers are eligible for retirement. Over time, the system "matures" as workers with pension coverage reach retirement age and the beneficiary/worker ratio rises. This ratio has increased dramatically in all the public plans (see Table 3–4). The federal systems are typically more mature than plans at the state-local levels where employment has grown dramatically. The relative maturity of the systems is reflected in the ratio of about 50 beneficiaries per 100 employees for the federal civil service and military compared to 14 beneficiaries per 100 state-local workers. The implication of the maturing process is that the required contributions for pensions will rise steadily until the beneficiary/worker ratio reaches equilibrium.

FUTURE COSTS

The maturation of the public pension systems will be one of the most important factors determining the level of future costs for public pension plans. Inflation and productivity growth will also play a significant role in the future level of public pension benefit expenditures. On the other hand, the projected demographic shifts, which are so important for the increasing costs of social security, have smaller implications for public plans.

Demographic Shifts and Employment Patterns

The costs of all programs targeted to assist the elderly have been projected to rise continuously through the first half of the 21st century. The increase in the relative share of social resources devoted to the aged reflects dramatic demographic shifts.

Persons age 65 and over represent an increasing proportion of our population. The number of persons age 65 and over has almost doubled since 1950 and is projected to increase through 2050. This trend is caused by several factors, the most important of which are a precipitous decline in the fertility rate and a significant increase in life expectancies.[5] In 1925, only 5 out of 100 people were 65 years or older. Today, 11 out of 100 people are in that age group, and by 2050, 16 out of 100 people will be 65 or over.[6]

The shift in the population's age structure has been accompanied by a decline in retirement ages. In recent years, about 55 percent of new social security retirees

---

4   Ibid.

5   Ibid., p. 137.

6   Shirley H. Rhine, *Older Workers and Retirement* (New York: The Conference Board, 1978), p. 22.

have selected early retirement at age 62 to 64 rather than remaining in the workforce until age 65.[7]

The changing demographic structure has important implications for the cost of the social security program. Although the system is mature, the beneficiary/worker ratio will be affected by the shift in the population profile. Because the program is essentially financed on a pay-as-you-go basis, costs are sensitive to the ratio of beneficiaries to workers. Today, there are 30 beneficiaries for each 100 workers, while in the year 2050 it is estimated that there will be 51 for each 100 workers. Since social security taxes are used directly to finance current benefits, the increase in beneficiary/worker ratio requires that payroll taxes be increased accordingly in order to pay the benefits.[8]

The application of nationwide demographic trends for projecting the future burden of public plans requires consideration of three issues: the impact of public pension costs for the general taxpayer; the employment trends for government workers; and the degree to which public pension systems are prefunded. The implications of these three factors are that demographic shifts are less important for public plans than for social security.

The bulk of public pension costs are ultimately paid by taxpayers. Although public employees contribute to their pensions, public plans are financed primarily by appropriations to the employing governmental unit. These appropriated funds come from tax revenues. Therefore, if increased funds are required to support pension expenditures, these funds will be collected from the entire taxpaying population. If all government programs were financed on a pay-as-you-go basis and if government employment were a constant percentage of total employment, then an aging population would necessitate higher taxes to support public employee pensions. Hence, it is necessary to consider trends in public employment and the extent to which the public plans are funded.

Employment growth trends at the various levels of government are quite disparate. At the federal level, a relatively stable workforce has evolved, while the number of state and local employees continues to rise. Civil service employment grew unevenly from 1950 to 1975, reflecting the onset and termination of two wars and the interest in space technology. Over the period, the annualized growth rate of employment was 1.3 percent. It is generally believed that the growth in civil service employment over the next quarter century will be slower, reflecting tightened government budgets and the stabilization of employment in the 1970s. Assuming that growth for 1975–2000 averages about one-half that of the 1950–75 period, or 0.6 percent per year, the federal government will employ approximately 3.3 million workers by the year 2000 (see Table 3–5).

Armed-forces employment increased during the 1960s reflecting the Vietnam War buildup. Since 1970, however, the military force has been gradually declining

---

7   *Social Security Bulletin*, Annual Statistical Supplement, 1975, Table 70, p. 98.

8   For further discussion of the impact of changing demography on social security costs, see Alicia H. Munnell, "Social Security," in *Setting National Priorities: The 1978 Budget* (Washington, D.C.: The Brookings Institution, 1977), Chapter 7.

Table 3-5.   Trends in Public Employment, 1950-75 and
Projections to 2000

| Year | Number of Workers (thousands) | | |
	Civil Service	Military	State and Local
1950	2,117	1,451	4,285
1955	2,378	2,923	5,054
1960	2,421	2,466	6,387
1965	2,588	2,644	8,001
1970	2,881	3,053	10,147
1975	2,890	2,117	12,097
1980	2,978	2,088	13,204[a] – 13,985[b]
1985	3,130	2,088	14,355 – 15,913
1990	3,209	2,088	15,594 – 18,030
1995	3,290	2,088	17,045 – 20,396
2000	3,339	2,088	18,509 – 22,801

[a] Projections based on increasing ratio of educational workers to population age 5 to 24 rising from 0.080 in 1975 to 0.136 in 2000 and constant ratio (0.047) of noneducational employment to population age 25 and over.

[b] Projections assume increasing ratios to population for both educational and noneducational employment. For education rising from 0.080 to 0.136 of population age 5 to 24 and for noneducational rising from 0.047 to 0.073 of population age 25 and over.

Source: Munnell and Connolly, "Funding Government Pensions," pp. 125, 126, 127.

in size. Assuming no major wars, military employment will probably remain relatively constant.

The state and local workforce has grown enormously, particularly since 1960. Because approximately one-half of state-local workers are engaged in education, a portion of this growth can be explained by the expansion of the school-age population. However, since the size of the school-age population has stabilized and is projected to decline, future growth of educational personnel will depend largely on increases in the teacher/pupil ratio. Noneducational employment in the state-local sectors has also grown significantly, reflecting the increased services required for a rising adult population. A continuation in the ratio of noneducational state-local employment to the population age 25 and over could result in total state-local employment increasing from 12 million persons in 1975 to 23 million by 2000. On the other hand, if the fiscal conservatism embodied in the California Proposition 13 issue becomes widespread, the ratio of public employees to population may stabilize.[9] In this case, total state-local employment may only increase to 18.5 million by 2000 (see Table 3-5).

---

9   In a 1978 referendum, California voters approved passage of Proposition 13 requiring a cutback in state property taxes. The move has precipitated a flood of similar bills in other states and has been interpreted as the beginning of a nationwide "taxpayer revolt."

Based on the estimates for the various plans, it appears that federal employment will most likely decrease as a percent of total employment, while state and local employment potentially could increase. Therefore, it is possible that the ratio of retired public workers to the working population would rise. However, the financial burden on the future working population depends on the degree to which the plans are funded. In actuarially funded plans, reserves are accumulated during the employee's worklife to finance retirement annuity. On average, state-local plans are characterized by considerable advanced funding; therefore, the major portion of increased costs will be paid annually.[10] In contrast, federal plans are financed virtually on a pay-as-you-go basis; thus, the deferred costs could represent a significant burden to future taxpayers. This burden, however, will be substantially mitigated because federal employment has stabilized, and so federal retirees will represent a decreasing portion of total retired workers.

In addition, pension costs for society as a whole and for public employees could be reduced substantially if retirement patterns changed. An increasingly popular proposal is the extension of the normal retirement age.

Reducing Long-run Costs by Extending Retirement Age.   Since reversal of the current demographic trends is neither likely nor socially desirable, relief from a surge in future tax rates must come from some other source. Later retirements would slow the rise in the beneficiary/worker ratio and shorten the period over which retirement benefits must be paid. A general increase in length of working life for the population as a whole would expand the tax base and soften the impact on tax rates of normal maturation of the plans.

Considering the improved health and life expectancy of today's elderly, it is more logical to prolong than to shorten their working life and to encourage active and productive employment beyond the customary retirement age of 65. Increased labor-force participation by the elderly who are physically able and who want to continue working would be beneficial to them, to the pension plans in which they participate, and to society as a whole. Many of the problems afflicting the elderly are related directly to the economic hardship caused by retirement, and naturally these would be relieved by earnings from continued employment. Working might also alleviate their isolation in a society that seems to have no place for them and restore their dignity and self-reliance. However, if the trend toward early retirement is ever to be reversed, measures that discourage the elderly from remaining in the workforce should be eliminated.

Impact of Recent Retirement Legislation.   The Age Discrimination in Employment Act was amended April 6, 1978 to remove mandatory retirement for federal employees and to increase the minimum mandatory retirement age from 65 to 70 for other private workers. Projecting the number of people who will stay on in public

---

10   Fully funded pensions will experience no increase in costs since the liability for maturing obligations has been previously offset through the accumulation of assets. Only if the actuarial assumptions on which previous contribution rates were based were erroneous would advance funded systems experience any additional costs from the shift in demography. However, since few public systems are fully funded, almost all systems experience an increase in cost when the number of beneficiaries rises. This is because these plans have deferred recognition of some portion of the pension liability until employees actually retire.

employment past age 65 due to the removal of the mandatory retirement provision is problematical.

The Civil Service Commission is required under the new law to study the federal employee provisions. The report is to be completed and transmitted no later than January 1, 1980. The Secretary of Labor is also requested to conduct a study focusing on the feasibility of raising the age limitation beyond 70 and of eliminating the upper age limit for all employees. An interim report is to be submitted by January 1, 1981 and the final report by January 1, 1982. It is difficult to predict what these studies will conclude because an individual's reasons for retirement are complex. However, most civil service experts expect little change in the number of persons retiring after age 65.

Studies based on the Social Security Administration's "Survey of Newly Entitled Beneficiaries" (1968) sample estimate that by 1985 the labor force will have increased by 375,000 members, only 1/3 of 1 percent, due to the change in mandatory retirement.[11] However, if changes in the social security retirement age are provoked by population pressures, workers may be encouraged to stay on beyond age 65. The 1977 Amendments to the Social Security Act have already extended (as of 1982) from 72 to 70 the age after which the earnings test is no longer applicable. The long-range effect of increasing the normal retirement age to 68 would be significant.[12]

Inflation and Productivity

Pension costs are extremely sensitive to changes in the rates of inflation and productivity growth. These factors impact on pension expenses in two ways. First, the increase in wages resulting from inflation or productivity growth raises the compensation base on which benefits are based. Second, plans with postretirement inflation adjustments necessarily raise the cost of pension annuities.

Wages rise to compensate workers for increases in productivity and inflation. Because pension benefits are usually related to wages, the value of workers' expected annuities also increases in response to productivity and inflation. However, since employees must contribute a fixed percentage of wages to the pension fund, plan revenues receive a boost when wages are raised. Whether or not the increase in employee contributions is sufficient to cover the cost of the higher benefits depends on the averaging period used in calculating the compensation base.

If benefits are based on final salary (or an average of the last few years of earnings), contributions will not be adequate to cover the benefit increase. While the compensation base reflects the total compound effect of all prior years' increases, contributions based on lower earnings do not reflect the full value of the increases incorporated into benefits. With career averaging, the increments in employee contributions exactly offset benefit increases (see Table 3–6). Because most public pensions are final-average plans, productivity and inflation raise the cost of pension benefits for the employer.

---

11   See Janice Halpern, "Raising the Mandatory Retirement Age: Its Effect on the Employment of Older Workers," *New England Economic Review* (May-June 1978), p. 31.

12   Ibid., pp. 33–34.

Table 3–6.   Effect of Salary Growth under Career-Average and Final-Salary Pension Systems

Cumulative Benefits Accrual	No Growth		Growth = 2%	
	Salary	Contribution	Salary	100% Contribution
1%	1,000	100	1,000	100.0
2	1,000	100	1,020	102.0
3	1,000	100	1,040	104.0
4	1,000	100	1,061	106.1
5	1,000	100	1,082	108.2
6	1,000	100	1,104	110.4
7	1,000	100	1,126	112.6
8	1,000	100	1,148	114.8
9	1,000	100	1,172	117.2
10	1,000	100	1,195	119.5
10%	10,000	1,000	10,948	1,094.8 Total

	No Growth		Growth = 2%	
	Final Salary	Career Average	Final Salary	Career Average
Compensation base	1,000	10,000/10 = 1,000	1,195	10,948/10 = 1,094.8
Replacement rate	10%	10%	10%	10%
Annual benefit	100	100	119.5	109.48
Assumed years of retirement	10	10	10	10
Total value benefits	1,000	1,000	1,195.0	1,094.8
Total value contributions	1,000	1,000	1,094.8	1,094.8
Surplus (deficit)	0	0	(100.2)	0

Source: Author's calculations.

Postretirement inflation adjustments raise the cost of pension annuities. Expenditures for current beneficiaries rise annually by the same percentage as the inflation adjustment, generating additional liabilities for the system. In addition, the expected cost of providing annuities to current workers' increases raises the normal cost of the plan.[13] The combined impact of these two effects can be substantial. Since most public employees are covered by plans providing automatic adjustments which at least partially compensate for cost-of-living increases, inflation is an important component of the escalation of public pension costs.

Despite the importance of productivity and inflation increases, many plans ignore expected wage increases and cost-of-living adjustments when calculating pension expenses. Use of static assumptions which understate pension costs is one way in which government employers may minimize the drain on current operating budgets while still satisfying statutory funding requirements.

Although the civil service retirement system prepares alternative estimates of plan costs based on dynamic assumptions, the system's annual payments to the fund are still calculated on a static valuation of plan costs. The House Pension Task Force has criticized this practice and urged the use of dynamic assumptions for calculation of the civil service retirement system's required annual contributions.

Although most experts agree that anticipated wage increases should be incorporated in the calculation of pension costs, some disagreement exists about the desirability of including postretirement inflation adjustments. Opponents of inclusion argue that attempts to recognize future cost-of-living increases would be unrealistic given the difficulty of predicting the future path of inflation. Any estimate of future wage or cost-of-living increases involves, in part, an assumption regarding the future rate of inflation.

Estimates of Future Costs

Precise estimates of the increase in the future tax burden implied by escalating pension costs are unavailable. However, some idea can be gleaned from rough projections of the future contribution rates which would be required if no change were made in the funding policies of public plans. 1976 estimates indicate that by the year 2000 the combined employer and employee contribution rate for state-local plans will increase from 11.8 to 15.4 percent of payrolls.[14] The increase for federal plans will be even more dramatic. Rates for the military will jump from 40.3 to 60.3 percent of payrolls, while federal civil service rates will increase from 21.5 to 30.6 percent of payrolls.

Contribution increases of this magnitude will be a significant drain on public funds. Unfortunately, the maturation of public pensions and the concomitant emergence of previously unrecognized pension expenses coincide with a growing

---

13   The normal cost is the amount which must be contributed in a given year to cover the cost of benefits earned in that year.

14   Alicia H. Munnell and Ann M. Connolly, "Funding Government Pensions: State-Local, Civil Service and Military," in *Funding Pensions: Issues and Implications for Financial Markets*, Conference Series No. 16 (Federal Reserve Bank of Boston, October 1976), Tables A-1, A-3, pp. 125-127.

resistance to tax increases, particularly at the state and local levels. It is yet unknown how the need for increased taxes to support pension payments will be balanced against other taxpayer demands for both tax reduction and increases in other services.

FUNDING

The area of pension plan funding is technically complex. Essentially, funding is an accounting issue concerning the appropriate timing of recognition of expenses. Although the methods of funding are as varied as are the number of accounting techniques, examination of the extremes will clarify the problem.

Pay-as-you-go financing is the equivalent of cash-basis accounting since expenses are not recognized until payment is due. No trust fund is accumulated and contributions exactly equal benefit payments in every year.[15] The required contribution for newly established pay-as-you-go systems is very small or even zero and grows steadily as the beneficiary/worker ratio rises.

Actuarially funded systems follow an accrual method of accounting. Expenses for benefit payments are recognized as pension rights are earned by employees. Contributions equivalent to the expected present value of benefits are made annually as pension obligations are incurred. This annual figure is referred to as the normal cost.[16] However, since pensions usually extend credits to employees for service rendered prior to the establishment of the plan, new pensions start out with a significant liability. In order to fund this obligation and others resulting from general liberalizations of plan provisions, supplemental payments are made to amortize the liability over a period of years—usually 30 or 40. Plans which have paid off the entire liability are fully funded while those which have not—or which fail to make payments equal to the true normal cost—are partially funded. As noted earlier, fully funded pensions experience no increase in required annual contributions as the beneficiary/worker ratio rises because the money to pay for maturing pension obligations has already been collected. Partially funded systems will of course experience some increase in the required contribution rate as the system matures, but the rise will be less dramatic than that for pay-as-you-go plans.

In addition to providing valuable information on the true costs of benefit provisions and equalizing the stream of pension expenditures, actuarial funding lowers the total contribution required. Because assets are accumulated and invested, interest income provides an important additional revenue source for funded systems. Thus, although funding may seem more costly than pay-as-you-go financing when plans are first established, full funding actually requires the least amount of employee and employer contributions.

---

15   Contributions under a pay-as-you-go system may exceed benefits in some years to provide for the buildup of a small contingency reserve.

16   Normal cost may be calculated according to a number of actuarial methods. In this discussion, entry-age normal costing which evens out the stream of payments to a level percent of pay will be assumed.

Table 3–7. Public-Employee Retirement System Funding Methods

Percent of Defined Benefit Plans

System category	Nonactuarial Basis			Actuarial Basis				
	Pay as You Go	Terminal Funding	Employer Matching or Other Non-actuarial Basis	Normal Cost Paid and No Unfunded Accrued Liability	Normal Cost Paid and Unfunded Accrued Liability Amortized Over 40 Years or Less	Payment Less than Normal Cost and 40-Year Amortization of Unfunded Accrued Liability	Unknown	Total
Federal government	34.8			7.0	44.2	14.0		100
State and local governments								
I. By level of administration								
State	23.1	1.2	4.5	7.8	45.0	14.1	4.5	100
Local	16.6	0.1	26.0	17.9	25.8	7.2	6.2	100
II. State and local totals by system coverage type								
State and local	16.3	0.1	5.5	24.0	42.3	5.3	6.4	100
Police and fire	16.6	0.2	31.2	15.6	22.2	8.2	5.8	100
Teachers (including higher education)	42.1	1.1	3.3	4.4	28.4	10.4	10.3	100
Total	17.0	0.2	24.7	17.4	26.8	7.7	6.1	100

Source: U.S. House of Representatives, Committee on Education and Labor, *Pension Task Force Report on Public Employee Retirement Systems*, 95th Cong., 2nd sess., March 15, 1978, Table 61, p. 151.

Table 3–8. Frequency of Public-Employee Retirement System Actuarial Valuations
(percent of defined benefit plans)

System Category	None in Last 10 Years	Valuation Made but Not on a Regular Basis	Valuation Made at Least Every 3 Years	Valuation Made Every 4 Years or More	Total
Federal government	34.0	2.1	59.6	4.3	100
State and local government by level of administration					
State	5.2	19.1	69.9	5.9	100
Local	25.1	15.2	53.2	6.4	100
Total	23.9	15.5	54.2	6.4	100

Source: *Pension Task Force Report*, Table 62, p. 158.

As Table 3–7 indicates, the funding methods used in the public sector cover the entire possible range. Although at least 42 percent of federal, state and local pensions are not actuarially funded, only 34.8 percent of federal and 17 percent of state-local systems—primarily plans for police and fire fighters—are on a pay-as-you-go basis. The rest of the nonactuarially funded systems accumulate reserves against future obligations but do not explicitly relate contributions to benefits as they accrue.

Nonactuarially funded plans with some accumulated reserve derive the benefit of investment revenue. However, without periodic valuations, actual pension costs are unknown and plan administrators cannot determine whether the system is over- or underfunded. Even some actuarially funded plans may be unaware of true pension costs because of the infrequency with which valuations are required. Table 3–8 indicates that only about one-half of public pensions have actuarial valuations every three years or less.

Infrequent valuation, use of static or otherwise unrealistic actuarial assumptions, and lack of uniformity in funding methods and definitions make it difficult to assess the degree of funding achieved by actuarially funded plans. For example, although 7 percent of federal and 17 percent of state-local plans indicate they have no unfunded liabilities, only about one-half of these are actually fully funded. This paradox is attributable to the fact that nearly one-half of the actuarially funded plans uses the aggregate-level cost method (without a supplemental liability) of actuarial valuation under which the unfunded liability is defined to be zero at all times.[17]

---

17   There are six major methods of actuarial funding of which aggregate and entry-age normal are two examples. For an explanation of actuarial methods and definitions, see Charles L. Trowbridge, "Fundamentals of Pension Funding," in *Transactions of the Society of Actuaries*, Vol. IV, No. 19. For an explanation of the aggregate-level cost methods with and without supplemental liability, see Dan M. McGill, *Fundamentals of Private Pensions*, Third Edition (Homewood, Ill.: Richard D. Irwin, Inc., 1975), pp. 358–362.

In the absence of an existing uniform measure of funding, the House Pension Task Force adopted the ratio of unfunded accrued liability to plan assets as a measure of funding status. A plan with a ratio of 100 percent would have sufficient funds on hand to pay off all promised benefits and therefore could be considered fully funded. Table 3–9, which presents the ratio of assets to accrued liabilities for large public systems, indicates that less than 5 percent of public plans approach full funding.

Another measure of the funding status of the public plans is provided by the amount of unfunded accrued liability. As of 1975, total unfunded liabilities of the civil service, military and state-local plans exceeded $600 billion. The estimates for civil service and the military are consistent with valuations prepared by actuaries for each system using similar wage, price and interest assumptions. The figure for aggregate state-local pensions is considerably higher than the $120 billion estimate in the *Pension Task Force Report*, although the *Report* acknowledges that the $120 billion may be understated by 20 to 30 percent because some state-local plans employ static assumptions.[18] Hence, the unfunded liability for state-local pensions probably falls somewhere between $150 billion and $270 billion. In any case, the unfunded liability in the public sector is substantial.

There is no general agreement on what standard is appropriate for measuring the adequacy of public pension funding. However, it seems reasonable that differences in taxing power between governmental units should be considered when evaluating the funding levels of federal, state and local plans.

Desirable Standards at the State-Local Levels

The appropriate funding of state-local pensions clearly falls in the broad area between the pay-as-you-go financing of social security and the rigid full funding requirements established for private pensions under ERISA. Some degree of funding is desirable at the state-local levels (1) to enforce fiscal responsibility through explicit recognition of the long-term costs of proposed benefit changes; (2) to ensure that adequate revenues are available to fulfill future pension obligations; (3) to allocate pension costs as benefits accrue so that they are financed by the generation that enjoys the services of public employees; and (4) to strengthen the position of state-local governments in financial markets to avoid excessive interest costs of low credit ratings due to large unfunded liabilities. However, unlike private plans, public systems are supported by governments which have perpetual life and the power of taxation; these characteristics substantially reduce the need for public plans to achieve a fully funded status.

The analogy to the federal government's power of taxation to finance social security on a current-cost basis as a rationale for pay-as-you-go financing at the state-local levels is misleading. The social security program differs fundamentally from state-local pensions. The revenue base to finance a pay-as-you-go system at the federal level is substantially broader and less sensitive to economic or natural disaster than that available to any state or municipality. The federal government's ability to pool economic risk ensures a stable stream of future revenues, while the future revenues of smaller governmental units are considerably less certain.

---

18 *Pension Task Force Report*, p. 165.

Table 3–9. Ratio of Plan Assets to Accrued Liability for Federal Systems and 70 Percent of Large State and Local Public-Employee Retirement Systems (percent of plans)

System Category	Ratio of Assets to Accrued Liability										
	10 or less	11 to 20	21 to 30	31 to 40	41 to 50	51 to 60	61 to 70	71 to 80	81 to 90	Over 90	Total
Federal	4.5		4.5	4.5	18.2	31.8	22.7	4.5	4.5	4.5	100
State and local (70 percent of large plans)	4.6	9.1	5.7	11.1	16.5	16.5	16.1	11.1	7.0	2.3	100
Largest 25 state and local plans			8.0	8.0	8.0	36.0	16.0	16.0	4.0	4.0	100

Source: *Pension Task Force Report*, Table 67, p. 164.

Table 3-10. Unfunded Accrued Liability of Public Plans, 1975

Program	Unfunded Liability (billions)[a]
Civil service	$164.3
Military	195.0
State-local	270.3[b]

[a] These estimates are based on the following economic assumptions: wage growth = 5 percent, interest = 6 percent, cost of living = 3 percent.

[b] This figure differs significantly from the $100–120 billion estimate of the House Pension Task Force. The wide variation in estimates of unfunded liability highlights the sensitivity of such figures to actuarial assumptions and methodology. Some of the difference in the two estimates can be explained by the fact that the lower estimate includes no provision for cost-of-living adjustments and that some state-local plans use static assumptions.

Source: Munnell and Connolly, "Funding Government Pensions," Table 20, p. 116.

Moreover, despite pay-as-you-go financing, the Social Security Administration projects long-term costs over a 75-year period. Every proposed change in the program is accompanied by a price tag reflecting the increased contribution (as a percentage of taxable payrolls) required to finance the benefit expansion. These projections serve as a disciplinary mechanism to prevent an extravagant expansion of the program which would unduly burden future generations.

While pay-as-you-go financing is not appropriate for public plans, neither are the rigorous funding standards ERISA requires for private plans. In addition to covering normal costs, single-employer private plans must amortize their unfunded liability over a 40-year period (30 years for plans established or liabilities created after January 1, 1974) and, in order to encourage realism in the choice of actuarial assumptions, experience gains and losses must be amortized over 15 years. The ERISA standards are the maximum funding requirements to be considered for public pensions.

Funding standards for state-local systems can be less rigorous as these governmental units are virtually perpetual entities. Although funding methods are available which avoid the distinction between normal costs and accrued liability, these two concepts are useful because they represent significantly different issues. Every argument points to at least covering normal costs. Accrued pension benefits represent an integral part of the compensation package of government workers, and these costs should be recognized explicitly and paid by the generation of workers that enjoys the services rather than deferred to future generations. These contributions ensure that reserves will accumulate for new employees equivalent to the value of the workers' pensions at the time they are expected to retire.

The more difficult issue is how to deal with the large unfunded liability that already has been amassed in the public pension sector (see Table 3-10). These liabilities cannot be ignored because they represent a significant claim on future revenues. This raises the possibility that future taxpayers might search for ways to

avoid the full impact of promised benefits. In addition, these large unfunded liabilities undermine the confidence of investors in state and local securities requiring
compensation through higher interest payments. Finally, ignoring past service liability will provide unrealistic price tags on benefit changes that do not affect normal
cost.

While a program of amortizing these liabilities over, for example, a 40-year
period would remedy all the deficiencies in this existing structure of state-local
pensions, practical difficulties exist in implementing such an ambitious scheme at
the state and local levels. First, funding requires large amounts of revenues, which
must be derived from higher taxes. If the $270 billion were amortized over 40 years
(as a level percentage of payrolls) beginning in 1975, the first-year payment would
amount to about $9.6 billion,[19] which would represent a 7 percent increase in total
state and local taxes.[20] As a more specific example, Massachusetts is in the process
of moving from a pay-as-you-go to a fully funded status. The full revenue impact
of the new funding scheme has been mitigated by a five-year transition mechanism;
however, if the amortization of the $7.6 billion unfunded liability had been intro-
duced in full in 1976, the annual payment of $315 million (which does not include
the $332 million required to cover normal costs) would have represented a 6 percent
increase in the 1976 tax bill for the Massachusetts state and local governments.[21]

Massachusetts is a good example of the potential hardship that can be imposed
by funding pension liabilities. The state already ranks among the highest in terms
of total taxes levied, and its economy was hit by the 1974–75 recession. Additional
taxes of $315 million to build up pension reserves represent an immediate net drain
on the Massachusetts economy. Prudent pension fund managers must invest these
funds where they can receive the highest return, and this means these funds most
likely will not be invested in Massachusetts industries.

The second difficulty with full funding is more political than economic in nature.
The accumulation of a large reserve might create its own pressure for expanding
the state's pensions and increasing benefits. This danger, however, seems less likely
now than in the past since the benefits of most state-local systems currently replace
a substantial percentage of earnings. Nevertheless, political pressures to spend
accumulated funds might arise, and consideration must be given to guard against
such a contingency regardless of the funding scheme adopted.

Because full funding is unnecessarily burdensome for states and localities, an
alternative is to freeze the unfunded liabilities at current levels and pay the accrued
pension benefits from general revenues as they become due. This approach would
require interest payments on the unfunded liability as well as the establishment of
a funding schedule (perhaps over 30 years) for any increase in the accrued liability

---

19   Munnell and Connolly, "Funding Government Pensions," Table 20, p. 116.

20   Total state and local taxes in the United States amounted to $129.4 billion in fiscal 1975. See *1977
Economic Report of the President* (Washington, D.C., January 1977), Table B–74, p. 273.

21   Massachusetts Retirement Law Commission, *The Actuarial Valuation Report of the Contributory
Retirement Systems of the Commonwealth of Massachusetts as of January 1, 1976*. State and local tax
receipts amounted to $5.2 billion in Massachusetts in fiscal 1976 (Department of Commerce, U.S. Bureau
of the Census).

resulting from liberalization of benefits. Requiring full funding of benefit changes that affect the accrued liability would offset the major disadvantage of "interest-only" funding: its tendency to underprice benefit liberalizations that affect accrued liabilities but not the normal cost. This approach, combined with covering normal costs, would result in fully funded public plans when the current generation of workers and retirees dies.

Freezing the unfunded liability and covering the normal costs should comprise the minimum funding requirements for state and local pensions. Naturally, the sponsors of public plans are free to adopt more rigid funding schedules if that were deemed desirable. However, these minimum standards would alleviate most of the concern about the long-run financial viability of state and local pensions. Any state or locality following minimum standards would be considered fiscally responsible, thereby avoiding excessive interest charges. Normal costs plus funding of additional accrued liability will ensure that all elements of long-term costs are taken into account. Contributions can be calculated as a level percent of payroll, thereby ensuring governments a steady stream of revenues. These minimum standards will moderate the large projected increase in costs which would result under pay-as-you-go financing as the ratio of beneficiaries to workers increases, and the interest earned on higher reserves will reduce total required contributions. At the same time, states and localities will have greater flexibility than under the funding standards for private pensions established under ERISA.

Issues in Funding the Military and Civil Service

If similar funding practices were adopted by federal plans, accumulation of reserves would not follow automatically. Unless total government taxes are increased or expenditures reduced by the amount required for the funding payment, the funding scheme will involve nothing more than a paper transaction between the Treasury and the civil service or the military retirement fund. For instance, if the annual contribution of $10 billion were required to fund civil service, the civil service retirement account could be credited every year with $10 billion and the Treasury account debited for the same amount. This intragovernmental transfer would not show up in the unified federal budget, and this is completely appropriate since no accumulation of government funds has occurred. After 40 years, the civil service retirement fund would appear to have accumulated $400 billion. Assume a decision is made at that time to pay off all accrued benefits. An expenditure of $400 billion would appear in the budget which would then have to be financed either by increased taxes or increased debt since no government fund had actually been accumulated (civil service assets are offset by Treasury liabilities). In other words, it is not sufficient to run a surplus in the civil service retirement account; funding requires a larger surplus or smaller deficit in the total federal budget.[22]

---

22   The same principle, of course, applies at state-local levels as well. To the extent that state and local pension plans hold as assets bonds of their respective governmental units, funding is illusory. However, since few state or local plans invest a significant portion of their assets this way, the problem is minimal for lower-level governmental units.

The magnitude of the federal deficit or surplus should not, however, be dictated by the funding practices of federal retirement plans. Flexibility in the orchestration of fiscal policy is essential to the achievement of macroeconomic goals. Therefore, application of funding requirements at the federal level appears fruitless.

Regular actuarial valuations based on realistic assumptions which account for anticipated wage and salary increases are, however, advisable. Accurate analysis of existing pension costs and the implications of proposed benefit changes is necessary to provide the public with an awareness of the full cost of public services and to check unwarranted benefit liberalizations.

Competing Claims in Public Budgets

The temptation for financially strapped employers to neglect funding payments is strong since the effects of inadequate funding will usually not be felt until the present group of public officials has left office. The ease with which funding payments can be avoided makes this method of reducing the drain of pension obligations on current operating budgets widespread.

The full fiscal impact of statutory funding requirements may be easily eroded by plan administrators who adopt overly optimistic actuarial assumptions. By underestimating the costs of future benefit payments, employers may reduce current pension obligations without appearing to transgress legal requirements. However, the effects of such manipulation will surface in the future when funds are insufficient to meet benefit obligations.

Plans which are unconstrained by legislative funding mandates have even more freedom to defer contributions. Since many such plans do not require regular actuarial valuations, the impact which present unsound financing will have on future taxpayers is frequently unrecognized.

Poor financial planning has occasionally resulted in default on pension obligations. However, due to the relative immaturity of most public plans, few government employers have yet been forced to face a direct tradeoff between the welfare of pensioners and the public's demand for current services. Nevertheless, there are instances of pension benefit reduction or termination by government employers who were unable or unwilling to divert operating revenues from other programs to finance annuity payments. For example, in 1972 the Hudson County New Jersey Employees Pension Fund was temporarily placed in receivership pending a bankruptcy declaration by the courts. The pensions of 240 persons were terminated by the court-appointed receiver. Temporary benefit suspensions have occurred in some of the local police and fire plans in Michigan, Arkansas, Mississippi, and Oklahoma.[23]

Rather than endangering the benefits of current beneficiaries, some systems have reduced the benefit amounts which active employees may expect at retirement. For instance, several plans in Colorado and Connecticut have reduced disability benefits payable to future annuitants.[24] Other plans have recognized that future

---

23   *Pension Task Force Report*, p. 97.

24   Ibid., pp. 96–97.

pension costs will exceed their ability to pay and have reduced benefits for newly hired employees.

Although more than 70 percent of federal, state and local employees are covered by plans which are bound constitutionally or legislatively from reducing benefits for current employees and beneficiaries, the strength of these legal provisions is ambiguous. Court rulings in Michigan, Illinois and Tennessee indicate that constitutional and other legal provisions may be inadequate to compel employers to meet current benefit payments or statutory funding requirements. Therefore, sound financial planning is the only vehicle that can ensure real security for employees covered by public pension plans.

SUMMARY

Millions of public employees and their families rely on government-sponsored pension plans to provide financial security in the event of death, disability or retirement. The financial capability of these plans to meet their obligations is therefore a matter of significant interest to both potential beneficiaries and the general public who support the plans through taxes.

Unfortunately, differences in the frequency of actuarial valuations as well as lack of uniformity in actuarial assumptions and methods make it impossible to derive any firm conclusions about the financial status of public pensions. However, it is fairly clear that most public systems are not fully funded and that a number continue to operate on a pay-as-you-go basis. To the extent that public pensions are not fully funded, they will experience an escalation in required contribution rates due to normal maturation of the plan exacerbated somewhat by recent demographic and retirement trends.

How the required increased taxes to finance burgeoning pension expenditures will be balanced against taxpayer demands for tax reductions and increases in other services remains to be seen. It is obvious, however, that the costs of the supplementary payments necessary to eliminate the massive unfunded liabilities already accrued by the public pension network will be very expensive. Full funding is, therefore, probably impractical for most systems. In any case, this degree of financial security may be excessive in view of the permanence of governmental units. Freezing of current unfunded liabilities through payment of interest, covering normal costs and actuarial prefunding of benefit liberalizations, may be a more reasonable standard of adequacy for state and local systems. Federal systems remain a dilemma since true funding would require increases in tax rates or reductions in overall government expenditures. In either case, there would necessarily be an undesirable amount of restriction on discretionary fiscal policy.

Regardless of the degree of funding adopted, regular valuations based on realistic economic assumptions are essential. Only this type of full information will allow the public and its representatives to make rational decisions about future benefit provisions.

4

Portability of Pension Credits

Through broad extension of compulsory OASHDI coverage the federal government has ensured the complete transferability of social security credits, thereby preserving the basic retirement protection of mobile workers throughout the private sector. Although most public workers are similarly protected, the 30 percent of state-local workers and federal civilian employees who lack social security coverage are exposed to gaps in retirement insurance. Even among workers covered by social security, geographic or occupational mobility may jeopardize an employee's retirement security since supplementary pension credits earned through participation in an employer-sponsored plan are rarely transferrable to a pension provided by a different employer.

While vesting provisions in federal, state-local and private plans provide some insurance against the risk of benefit loss, this is only a partial solution. The lack of portability limits the ability of even final earnings plans to compensate the worker for increases in wages and prices over a working life. Final-average earnings plans use a higher compensation base and therefore usually provide higher benefits than career-average plans because they reflect the compound effect of all productivity and inflation increases occurring during the worker's career. However, deferred pension benefits for terminated vested employees are based on compensation at the time the employee shifted jobs and therefore exclude increases in wages and prices occurring between termination of employment and retirement. As a result, deferred benefits are frequently closer to career-average benefits which are less generous because of the inclusion of the generally lower early years of earnings in the compensation base. Consider a worker who enters the labor force at age 25 and changes jobs every 10 years until the employee retires at age 65. Even if each of the worker's employers sponsors a final earnings plan and the benefits are fully vested, the final pension will resemble that of a career-average plan. Table 4–1 presents a simple example of the difference in pension benefits between a worker with a continuous earnings history with one employer and a worker who shifts jobs in mid-career. In periods of rising wages, without portability the mobile employee will always end up with a lower pension benefit.

Limited portability is available in the private sector. Multiemployer plans were designed to provide continuous coverage for workers who frequently changed jobs within a given industry. In general, however, no mechanism exists for transferring pension credits between plans.

In the public sector, considerable portability is available for workers who transfer employment within a particular governmental unit. However, only social security coverage and vesting protect those workers who transfer between units of government or from public to private employment. Furthermore, lack of coordination between the major federal plans—civil service and the military—has created the

Table 4-1. Comparison of Pension Benefits for a Single-Job and a Dual-Job Worker
with 30 Years of Employment

Year	Salary[a]	Average of High Five Years	Replacement Percent[b]		Benefit		
			Single-Job Worker	Dual-Job Worker	Single-Job Worker	Dual-Job[c] Worker	
1	$ 3,470						
6	4,651						
7	4,884						
8	5,128	$ 5,140		20		$1,028	
9	5,384						
10	5,653						
26	12,341						
27	12,958						
28	13,605	$13,638	60	40	$8,183	$5,455	
29	14,286						
30	15,000						
					$8,183	$6,483	Total

[a] Assumes annual wage growth of 5 percent.

[b] Assumes unit benefit accrual of 2 percent per year.

[c] Assumes employee works 10 years at first job and 20 years at second job.

Source: Author's calculations.

potential for double dipping whereby government workers become eligible for two annuities for the same period of coverage or qualify for a military pension while receiving a government salary.

FEDERAL PLANS

The federal civil service retirement system and the federal uniformed services plan are by far the most important pension plans maintained by the federal government for its employees. All members of the armed forces are automatically covered by the military plan and social security, and 90 percent of federal civilian employees are insured under the civil service system. As noted in Chapter 1, a variety of other federal pensions exists to provide retirement security for the remaining groups of civilian employees. Depending on how broadly federal employment is defined, as many as 68 different pensions may be considered federal staff plans. Of these, besides the civil service and military plans, six are of major significance: the Tennessee Valley Authority Plan, the District of Columbia Teachers Plan, the District of Columbia Police and Fire Plan, the Board of Governors of the Federal Reserve System Plan, the Foreign Service Plan, and the Central Intelligence Agency Plan.

Relationship between Civilian Staff Plans

In general, pension credits are portable among the different federal staff plans. The federal civil service provides a service credit purchase option to employees transferring from federal employment covered by another civilian staff plan.[1] An employee may receive full credit under the civil service system for other federal civilian employment provided that the worker withdraws his own contributions from the pension plan of the previous federal employer and redeposits those contributions in the civil service retirement account.[2] The second stipulation of credit transfer is that the employee must forfeit all rights to a pension from the previous employer for the same period of employment. Since forfeiture of vested rights to the employer-financed portion of benefits is automatic when an employee withdraws his own contributions from a federal plan, this is no problem.[3] One pension based entirely on the provisions of the civil service plan is awarded at retirement.

In most cases, the credit purchase arrangement is optional for the employee. However, credit transfer is mandatory and automatic for employees transferring from the CIA to the civil service. According to a special arrangement between the two systems, the employee's contributions as well as the contributions made by the CIA on the worker's behalf are automatically shifted from the CIA fund to the civil service account. The employee gets full credit for CIA service and receives a civil service annuity at the time of retirement. The agreement is reciprocal so that automatic transfer occurs in the same manner for employees shifting from civil service to CIA employment.

Although most major staff plans reciprocate by extending credit purchase options to workers transferring from civil service employment, there are exceptions. For instance, civil service credits are not portable to the TVA staff plan.[4] However, an employee shifting from civil service to the TVA who has less than a three-day break in service between the two positions may retain civil service coverage.[5] Such an employee is excluded from the TVA program and credits that employment directly to the civil service plan. Workers who have more than a three-day lapse between leaving civil service and joining the TVA must enroll in the TVA plan as new employees without credit for prior government service. At retirement, the employee receives

---

1   Civil service's portability policy with regard to other federal civilian plans is described in Civil Service Commission Pamphlet #18, "Your Retirement System" (Washington, D.C., July 1975), p. 7.

2   Employee contributions must also include interest earned since the time of original deposit.

3   Most federal plans contain a buy-back provision entitling employees to repurchase forfeited pension rights by redepositing their own contributions plus interest. However, civilian employees may never receive credit for the same employment from more than one government system at a time.

4   TVA is the most significant program lacking portability provisions; however, some other smaller programs also deny credit for service with a different federal employer.

5   The three-day break in service provision is a civil service regulation which usually applies only when a civil servant shifts jobs between agencies which are both covered by civil service. This maintains continuity and avoids the necessity of withdrawing and reentering when the lapse in service is short. By special provision the same treatment is extended civil servants who transfer to TVA.

two pensions: one from the TVA based on service with that agency and a deferred benefit from the civil service, provided the employee's pension was vested and the employee did not withdraw his own contributions at the time of transfer.

For most transfers between civil service and another federal staff plan, however, portability is available. In addition, the same service credit purchase options are generally available to workers transferring among other major federal staff plans. Thus, federal civilian workers are protected in two ways. Because the majority of federal positions are covered by civil service, continuous protection under a uniform plan is assured for most mobile workers. Workers shifting to positions not covered by civil service are protected by portability arrangements between most federal programs. Although gaps and inconsistencies do occur, they affect only a small minority of employees.[6]

Relationship between the Military and Civil Service

Although the federal uniformed services plan does not recognize federal civilian employment, most federal staff plans provide credits for periods of military service. With few exceptions the major staff plans treat military service in the same way as the civil service plan does.[7]

The provisions governing creditation of military service by the civil service retirement plan are among the most complex portability arrangements found in government.[8] The unique characteristics of the military plan, including long vesting periods, low normal retirement age, and distinctions between reserve and regular officers, make it difficult to devise a simple credit transfer system between the military and civilian plans.

Since 20 years of service are necessary before an employee is eligible to receive a military pension, many individuals who have served in the armed forces have credits under the military plan which are insufficient to entitle them to a pension.

---

6   One curious inconsistency noted by the Comptroller General involves the Federal Reserve system plans. Although credits are mutually portable between the civil service plan and the Board of Governors of the Federal Reserve system plan, no portability exists between civil service and the retirement plan separately administered for employees of the regional Federal Reserve Bank. As a result, a civil servant who transfers to the Board and who has also worked for a Federal Reserve Bank may obtain credit for his or her entire career because the Board recognizes both Bank and civil service employment. However, persons who have worked at both the Board and a Bank can never receive civil service credit for Federal Reserve Bank employment. See Report to Congress by the Comptroller General of the United States, *Federal Retirement Systems: Unrecognized Costs, Inadequate Funding, Inconsistent Benefits* (Washington, D.C., August 1977).

7   The major exceptions are the TVA and the Board of Governors of the Federal Reserve system. The TVA credits only military service which interrupts the employee's TVA employment. The Board of Governors of the Federal Reserve system retirement plan automatically credits military service which does not lead to a military pension. However, former military personnel who are eligible for retired pay may not waive their military pension and credit their service toward the Board's retirement plan as is permitted in the civil service system. (See text for a discussion of waiver policy under civil service.)

8   Provisions governing creditation of military service by the civil service retirement plan are contained in Title V of the U.S. Code.

Such individuals, if subsequently covered under civil service, receive credit for their military tenure. Double counting of credit for the same service is not a problem because pension benefits will not be forthcoming from the military. Since the military plan is noncontributory, employees transferring from the military to civil service are exempted from the usual requirement of purchasing past service credit by depositing contributions made to the former employer's plan. Instead, Treasury reimburses civil service for the additional costs resulting from extensions of credit for military service.

To conform with the principle that employees should not receive credit from more than one federal retirement system for the same period of employment, years of social security coverage may be deducted from the employee's service history. Beginning in 1957, mandatory social security coverage was extended to the armed forces. As a result, persons with military service after 1956 contributed to and received earnings credits under social security. If the employee's military service plus other covered employment are sufficient to entitle that worker to a social security benefit, all years of military employment after 1956 are excluded by civil service and credit is given only for years prior to 1957. However, the social security exclusion is not applied until the retiree attains age 62, the earliest age at which social security retirement benefits are payable. Individuals eligible to receive a social security benefit because of prior military and other covered service who retire before age 62 receive a civil service benefit based on all years of military and civil service employment. When the retiree reaches age 62, civil service benefits are recomputed excluding years of military service after 1956.[9]

Former military employees whose armed-forces service is sufficient to entitle them to a nondisability military pension are not given credit for any years of military service under the civil service retirement plan. Such employees enter the civil service plan as new employees and accrue retirement credits according to the usual schedule beginning with the lower-unit accrual rates applicable to short-service employees. Upon retirement from civil service, the employee receives a civil service pension based only on civilian employment in addition to a military pension based on service in the armed forces.

Civil service does, however, have a special provision permitting employees who are eligible for military retired pay to transfer service credits to the civil service retirement plan. At the time of retirement from civil service, the employee may opt to waive rights to a military pension. All years of military service (except those after 1956 if the retiree is 62 and entitled to a social security benefit) are then credited toward a civil service pension, and the retiree receives retirement benefits only from the civil service plan. At present, this is the preferred option among civil servants retiring with rights to a military pension. For many such employees, inclusion of military service is necessary to bring the worker's total creditable service up to the minimum required for an early retirement option. For example, an employee who transfers to civil service from the armed forces at age 45 with 20 years of military service must include years of armed-forces employment to qualify for optional retirement at age 55 with 30 years' service.

---

9   Civil service benefits are recomputed when the retiree reaches age 62 regardless of whether or not the individual chooses to receive actuarially reduced early retirement benefits from OASDHI.

Double Dipping: Receipt of Two or More
Federal Pensions

Considerable attention has been devoted to the issue of "double dipping" by former military personnel who join the civil service. As it relates to the military, the term double dipping describes two distinct practices: receipt of more than one federal pension or receipt of a federal salary while drawing a federal pension.

Annuity-Annuity. There is nothing objectionable about receipt of more than one federal pension unless both pensions are based on credits earned for the same employment. The provisions governing portability among the federal civilian staff plans and between civilian plans and the military were specifically designed to avoid double crediting the same employment. Thus, none of the service credit transfers so far described provide an opportunity for pension double dipping—known as an annuity-annuity dip. However, there are two instances in which double crediting for military service does occur.

Persons who have been retired from the military because of disability may be allowed to credit military service to a federal civilian plan without waiving rights to their military pensions. If the disability was incurred while in active combat, civil service will automatically credit the individual's years of military service toward a civil service pension without requiring waiver of the disability benefits. At retirement, the worker may collect a civil service benefit based partially on military service in addition to a military benefit based on the same armed-forces employment.

Reserve officers who work for the civil service may also receive dual credits for military service. Even though reserve officers receive military credit for time spent fulfilling their annual active duty requirements, the civil service will credit the same active duty time toward a civilian pension. Thus, reserve officers may retire with a military pension and social security, in addition to a civil service pension based partially on the same armed-forces employment.

It is not known exactly how prevalent annuity-annuity dipping is or how much this practice costs the federal government. One of the tasks of the recently established President's Commission on Pension Policy will be to gather the relevant statistics on annuity-annuity dipping. Despite the attention this practice has received, it is most likely that this form of double dipping will be found far less costly than salary-annuity dipping.

Salary-Annuity. The potential for salary-annuity dipping arises from the provisions of the uniformed services plan which allow military personnel to retire at a young enough age to pursue a full second career.[10] Military employees may retire after 20 years of service, which means that most employees are only in their mid-40s when they retire from the service. Since military pension benefits commence

---

10   Salary-annuity dipping is not limited to military personnel. Lack of coordination in normal and early retirement-age provisions of federal civilian plans also opens the way for this form of double dipping by civilian personnel. However, since the military is believed to be the most serious case and since the problem is best illustrated by this example, the following discussion will focus on coordination problems with the uniformed services plan.

immediately, retired military personnel who assume a second career in federal civilian employment draw both a federal salary and a federal annuity simultaneously.[11]

The reason given for early military retirements is that it keeps the armed forces young and vigorous and facilitates rapid promotion by removing superannuated officers. The military retirement system has been consciously designed to complement the armed-forces promotion policy.

The early retirement provision of the military plan complements the armed-forces up-or-out promotion policy and stimulates advancement opportunities for younger officers by forcing into retirement older officers who have been passed over twice for a promotion. However, there is some question about the effectiveness of early retirement as an instrument for paring away deadweight. Data presented by the President's Commission on Military Compensation indicate that the 20-year vesting requirement constrains personnel managers because of reluctance to deprive employees of pension annuities.[12] Table 4–2 indicates that only a small percentage of military personnel are discharged involuntarily. As a result, officers who are not considered to have the potential for promotion to the next grade are retained at their current level until they complete 20 years of service and retire voluntarily.[13] This practice is clearly inconsistent with the principle of an up-or-out promotion policy.

The option of voluntary retirement after 20 years strips the manager of effective control over separations after this point. Retention of desired employees becomes a problem because many workers choose the 20-year retirement. Fifty-six percent of officer retirees and 77 percent of enlisted retirees have 22 or fewer years of service.[14]

Employees' perceptions of opportunities for a civilian career at 20 years of service and later at 30 years of service as well as their expectations for promotion influence the decision to terminate after 20 years. Since employment opportunities are superior for younger workers, most military personnel opt for early retirement rather than deferring assumption of a civilian career until they are forced into retirement upon completion of 30 years of service. If employees were permitted to remain in active service beyond their early 50s, the emphasis on securing a civilian position after military retirement might decline. However, under the current system,

---

11   The Dual Compensation Act of 1964 limits the total compensation which a retired regular officer can draw from the federal government. The salary of regular officers working in federal civilian employment is reduced by one-half of their annuity in excess of $4,532.06 as of September 1, 1978. (The offset breakpoint was originally set at $2,000 and is subject to semiannual adjustment.) Retired enlisted personnel and reserve officers are exempted from the offset provision, however. It is interesting that far more reserve officers than regular officers work in federal civilian jobs.

12   See *Report of the President's Commission on Military Compensation* (Washington, D.C., April 1978), Chapter 3.

13   Because the customary interval between promotions at the higher officer grades is 6 to 8 years, a person who received his or her final promotion after 12 years of service may remain until completion of 20 years of service even though it is clear the employee lacks desired leadership skills.

14   *Report of the President's Commission on Military Compensation*, p. 45.

Table 4–2.   Involuntary Separations in Fiscal Year 1976[a]

Years of Service	Enlisted Persons		Officers	
	Number of Involuntary Separations	Percent Involuntarily Separated[b]	Number of Involuntary Separations	Percent Involuntarily Separated[b]
5–9	7,337	2.9	402	0.6
10–14	1,107	0.8	1,157	2.6
15–19	320	0.2	476	1.0
Total (5–19)	8,764	1.5[c]	2,035	1.2[c]

[a] These data represent the number of personnel who were officially discharged with involuntary separation. There are probably more people who were involuntarily separated, but not coded as such.

[b] These percentages equal:

$$\frac{\text{Number involuntarily separated}}{\text{Total number on active duty with indicated years of service}} \times 100$$

[c] The weighted average of yearly percentages.

Source: Defense Manpower Data Center data as used in the *Report of the President's Commission on Military Compensation* (Washington, D.C., April 1978), Table 3–10, p. 45.

provision of an immediate pension annuity after 20 years speeds the exodus of highly qualified officers as well as those who are less qualified. Inability to retain some very talented personnel is a direct outgrowth of the design of the retirement program.

Linkage of retirement and promotion policy has been criticized as an inefficient method of achieving the desired personnel profile. Early retirement is viewed by some as an unnecessarily costly method of achieving personnel objectives. The President's Commission on Military Compensation has suggested that "retention, performance and morale can be stimulated by other compensation elements such as bonuses, and by noncompensation means such as effective leadership at all levels, sound training and assignment policies, enlightened design of jobs. . . ."[15]

Separation of retirement and promotion policy objectives would make possible a redesign of the uniformed services plan. More conventional vesting and retirement-age policies would help eliminate some of the salary-annuity dipping problems created when retired military personnel enter federal civilian employment. In line with this, the President's Commission on Military Compensation has recommended that conventional vesting provisions similar to those of the civil service retirement

15   Ibid., p. 56.

plan be employed by the military. Vested employees terminating prior to 20 years of service would be entitled to collect a deferred benefit at age 62.[16] Employees retiring with 20 to 29 years of service would receive a full benefit upon attainment of age 60 while workers with 30 or more years of service could collect an annuity at age 55 (just as under civil service regulations). The combination of vesting and deferred benefits would facilitate integration with civil service and reduce the possibility of double dipping.

Uniform Retirement Plan for All Federal Employees

More radical recommendations have been made to cope with the problems of coordinating the complex network of federal pensions, including consolidating all federal systems into a single retirement plan with uniform provisions. Proponents of such a scheme cite numerous inconsistencies and gaps in benefit protection resulting from the haphazard development of independent systems, and they conclude that equity considerations and management efficiency objectives would be forwarded by merging all plans. Special provisions could be incorporated in the plan to accommodate the needs of the minority of military personnel who are involved in hazardous employment. The balance of federal workers would be protected by provisions essentially the same as those presently covering federal civil servants. Naturally, consolidation of plans would eliminate any of the portability problems currently existing in federal employment.

STATE AND LOCAL PLANS

Although ERISA vesting requirements do not apply to public plans, most government pensions meet the minimum length-of-service standards.[17] However, vested benefits are affected by the contributory feature in public plans. Large numbers of employees withdraw their own contributions when they change jobs and thereby lose their vested benefits. The presence of relatively few terminated vested employees on public deferred pension rolls indicates that most vested participants do withdraw their contributions when leaving the plan.[18] Furthermore, 30 percent of

---

16   To protect the value of deferred benefits, the compensation base would be adjusted for changes in the cost of living occurring between time of separation and receipt of pension. Furthermore, to ease the transition to civilian life, generous severance pay would be available immediately to all terminated military personnel.

17   The *Pension Task Force Report* estimates that 44 percent of federal employees and 20 percent of state and local employees have either no vesting or later vesting than ERISA minimums. However, almost all of these employees are police, fire or military workers whose pension systems have many distinctive characteristics because of the unorthodox nature of the employment covered. U.S. House of Representatives, Committee on Education and Labor, *Pension Task Force Report on Public Employee Retirement Systems*, 95th Cong., 2nd sess., March 15, 1978, pp. 87–88.

18   Ibid., pp. 74–77, pp. 90–91.

state and local employees are not covered by social security and therefore may leave public employment without any pension credits for their government employment. Since the value of forgone benefits is frequently substantial, the widespread forfeiture of employer-financed benefits is believed to be a consequence of the generally inadequate reporting and disclosure practices of public plans. Thus, forfeiture requirements coupled with poor pension reporting have weakened the effectiveness of vesting as a protection against benefit reduction for public workers.

Nonvested employees in the public sector are also exposed to greater benefit loss than private-sector workers. Although private-sector plans must refund interest on employee contributions when withdrawn, nearly 50 percent of the plans covering almost 18 percent of state and local employees do not pay interest on refunded employee contributions. Even more serious, over 12 percent of local police and fire fighters are covered by plans which do not permit refund of mandatory employee contributions if the worker leaves before retirement.[19]

Intrastate Portability

It makes little sense for state retirement systems to penalize an employee who shifts from one form of state (or local) employment to another when both are covered by a state-enacted retirement law. Although job transfers may be voluntary, motivated by the worker's personal objectives for career advancement or to accommodate a working spouse who has been transferred, changes frequently are precipitated by state action such as agency reorganization or need for a redistribution of resources to provide more effective service to the public. In either case, lack of portability may impede mobility especially for older workers. To cope with this problem, many states have developed methods other than vesting to assure portability of pension credits. Nearly 82 percent of state and local employees are covered by plans permitting some form of intergovernmental portability.[20] However, there is considerable variation in the provisions of portability schemes.

Unilateral Credits. A small number of state and local government employees (3 percent) participate in plans which automatically credit service rendered another government employer without requiring either the employee or the former employer to contribute or reciprocate in some manner. A far more common portability arrangement allows employees the option of purchasing past service credit. Twenty-four percent of state and local workers may receive credit for prior in-state public employment if they pay some or all of the benefit cost of the service credit transfer. Teachers are most likely to be covered under such a scheme—70 percent of local public school teachers and 13 percent of the teaching staffs of public colleges and universities may purchase both in-state and out-of-state service credits.[21]

---

19   Less than 3 percent of the total number of state and local employees are covered by plans containing an ERISA-like provision prohibiting the forfeiture of vested benefits at the time an employee withdraws his or her own contributions. See Ibid., p. 90.

20   Ibid., p. 92.

21   Ibid., p. 93.

Reciprocity.   Reciprocal agreements between two or more retirement systems also provide portability for public employees. Over 70 percent of state-local workers are covered by plans having reciprocal agreements with one or more plans within their respective states.[22]

Although reciprocal arrangements take many forms, funds transfer schemes are the most common.[23] The New York system provides one example of how funds transfer arrangements work. In New York, when an employee transfers credits from one system to another, an appropriate reserve is shifted from the first system to the second. The employee's benefit is then calculated as though that worker had always participated in the second pension.

Unfortunately, differences in funding and in the actuarial bases for computing reserves make funds transfer schemes impractical between many systems. Intrastate agreements which prorate benefit costs on the basis of length of service in each system for retirees who have accumulated service under more than one plan are sometimes used instead. However, prorating involves considerable negotiations between plans to mesh systems if pension provisions are not identical in both plans. Fortunately, the need to design complex interplan portability arrangements has been somewhat relieved by the trend toward consolidation of retirement systems.

Consolidated Plans.   Nearly 75 percent of state and local workers participate in multiemployer plans which provide service credits for employment in any position within the system.[24] Merger of plans makes development of portability provisions unnecessary; however, similar types of problems may have to be worked out if the individual plans retain their distinctive provisions after consolidation. Whether benefits should be calculated according to the last plan's formula, or a combination of the formulas for the plans in which the employee has participated, and how costs should be allocated among plans are questions which must still be faced in consolidated systems.

The scope of the consolidated system may extend to all public employment within the state, although typically it is much more limited. Usually, statewide systems do not include local plans, leaving unresolved the problem of portability for municipal workers. Citywide systems encompassing all the plans in a municipality provide some measure of portability for local workers who shift occupations within the same town; however, geographically mobile workers or those who shift between levels of government are unaffected. In some cases, retirement plans covering employees within an occupational group may be consolidated throughout a state, thereby facilitating geographic but not occupational mobility. Thus, consolidation may ease the portability problem, but only in rare instances are statewide systems extensive enough to solve completely the problem of intrastate portability.[25]

---

22   Ibid. Such agreements are more than twice as common at the state level than at the local level (20.8 percent versus 8.3 percent).

23   Ibid. Fifty-five percent of reciprocal agreements require a transfer of funds between systems.

24   Ibid., p. 95.

25   Hawaii is one notable example of an all-inclusive statewide system which provides complete intrastate portability for public employees.

Despite a multiplicity of arrangements facilitating certain types of mobility (e.g., occupational or geographic), complete intrastate portability remains the exception rather than the rule. Even rarer are arrangements which permit pension credit portability between states.

Interstate Portability

Unlike public employees who shift jobs within the same state system, workers who transfer between states or between a state and the federal government actually change employers. Such workers are more likely to be exposed to the portability problems facing private-sector workers who change firms than employees who remain in-state.

In some instances, it is impossible or undesirable for workers to remain within a particular state. Many broad governmental programs—among them health, education and agriculture—are either joint federal and state projects or require employees to shift from one governmental jurisdiction to another. Under these circumstances, it is unfair to insist that the employee forfeit pension rights. Even if the nature of the worker's job does not require intergovernmental transfer, exchange of skilled personnel between states or between a state and the federal government may be in the best interests of the public. In recognition of this fact, some states have attempted to facilitate the interchange of employees by arranging for pension credit portability.

Some of the same methods used to establish portability within a state are available for creating interstate portability. Consolidation of plans, however, is not a solution since agreement by all states on a nationwide system of public plans is unlikely.

Service credit purchase arrangements are available to some types of workers. Teachers are most likely to be able to purchase credits. As previously mentioned, 70 percent of local public school teachers and 13 percent of the teaching staffs of public colleges and universities have this option. Overall, however, interstate service credit transfers are rare—only 9.2 percent of state and local workers are extended this option for out-of-state service.[26]

Reciprocal agreements have been worked out between some states. New York has been particularly active in seeking reciprocity with other states. However, many less affluent states are reluctant to enter into reciprocal agreements which may facilitate an outflow of experienced personnel to states which can afford higher compensation for their employees.

As a result of the difficulty of negotiating portability arrangements which are mutually acceptable to the states involved, interstate portability is rare. Workers transferring to the federal government are accorded even less benefit security. As a rule, portability between federal and state employment is nonexistent. Extension of credit for military service is the major exception. Approximately one-third of state and local plans covering 90 percent of all employees have various provisions giving

---

26   *Pension Task Force Report*, p. 93.

employees pension credit for periods of employment interrupted by military service.[27]

In short, unlike federal employees who have considerable portability mechanisms, state and local workers are generally able to transfer credits only within a state system. Transfers between states and the federal government are generally impossible.

SUMMARY

The need for flexibility in the transfer of personnel has stimulated the development of portability schemes by government employers. Arrangements specifically designed to ensure transfer of pension credits are far more prevalent in the public sector than in private industry. However, the extent of benefit security upon job transfer is uneven.

At the state and local levels, employees transferring between states or between levels of government are rarely afforded the opportunity to transfer pension credits. The paucity of portability arrangements affecting workers who shift employers in this way reflects the difficulty involved in negotiating mutually acceptable arrangements between plans with widely differing designs. Also, the reluctance of employers to facilitate the transfer of desired personnel plays a role very similar to that in private industry where portability agreements are rare.

In contrast, workers transferring between agencies within the same state or within the federal government are quite likely to have portability protection. Consideration of the inequity of penalizing workers who transfer jobs while effectively remaining in the service of the same employer has been partially responsible for the development of extensive networks of federal and intrastate portability arrangements.

In general, these arrangements have been successful in facilitating the exchange of personnel within agencies of the same governmental unit. However, at the federal level, some curious gaps and inconsistencies exist marring the efficiency of the system and in some cases creating an opportunity for annuity-annuity dipping. Similar problems exist at the state-local levels. The lack of completely inclusive systems of portability leaves certain workers unprotected and is the most serious deficiency at lower levels of government. Overall, however, portability within a governmental unit is fairly well established.

---

27   Ibid., p. 95.

5

Hazardous Employment

The military at the federal level and police and fire fighters at the state-local levels represent unique groups of workers without exact counterparts in the private sector. Many workers in the uniformed services hold jobs involving arduous physical tasks and therefore have special pension requirements. At each level of government, pension plans with characteristics distinct from those for general employees have been designed to yield a young and vigorous workforce. As a result, the military and police and fire plans share many common features such as long vesting, early retirement age and generous benefits. Because of these features, pension plans for workers in hazardous employment have become extremely expensive. The high costs and early retirement provisions have resulted in increased scrutiny of these plans to determine whether the existing provisions represent the most effective means of attaining the desired workforce.

Among the major issues are the comparability of compensation with civilian employees, the tradeoff between higher wages, larger pensions and early retirements, and cost control of compensation for these employees.

COMPARISON WITH OTHER PAY SYSTEMS

A comparison of compensation of the military, police and fire fighters with that paid civilian workers provides a useful benchmark. In general, total compensation for protective services appears superior to that of civilian employees especially when pensions are considered. However, higher pay for these groups of workers does not necessarily mean they are overcompensated since the additional compensation may be required to attract qualified workers.

Military

The current retirement system provides no benefits to workers who leave the armed forces with fewer than 20 years of service. Members with 20 years or more receive a lifetime annuity equal to 2.5 percent of basic pay for each year of active service. Hence, the annuity after 20 years is 50 percent of terminal basic pay rising to a maximum of 75 percent after 30 years. However, as discussed in Chapter 3, basic pay is only part of total salary so that if the replacement rates were expressed as a percent of regular military compensation (a proxy for total salary), the typical enlisted person would receive 35 percent after 20 years of service and about 57 percent after 30 years.[1] Benefits are increased automatically twice annually in line with accumulated changes in the consumer price index.

The military pension has figured importantly in comparisons of compensation with civilian employees. An analysis by the Rand Corporation, which compared 1974 total military compensation with compensation received in the same year by private-sector workers of similar age and education, concluded that military personnel earn significantly more than their average counterparts in the private sector.[2] The importance of the pension is highlighted by the fact that regular military compensation of enlisted personnel was quite close to median salaries of white high-school graduates of similar ages employed full time in the private sector. Salaries at senior levels (more than 20 years of service) were somewhat higher, indicating that the military paid a premium for qualified personnel. However, once the value of retirement and other benefits was added, the total compensation of military personnel was 30 to 50 percent above the median in the private sector.

The Rand study also compared officers' salaries with earnings of white college graduates and concluded that their pay was 20 to 40 percent above the median in private employment. Adding retirement and other benefits increased the differential dramatically. At every career point, total compensation for officers was 70 to 100 percent higher than the median total compensation in the private sector.

While the Rand study compared military and private-sector pay, a 1977 report of the Senate Appropriations Committee compared total compensation for specific military grades with compensation of federal civilian white-collar workers in comparable grades. This comparison revealed that total earnings of military personnel generally exceed civil service compensation although the magnitude of differential varied by rank. The premium for military ranged from a few percentage points to as much as 57 percent. However, in some of the low officer grades, military personnel fell slightly below their white-collar counterparts.[3] These results are supported by another comparison which found military compensation 3 to 22 percent higher for five of the six grades compared. Again, military compensation was slightly lower at the officer grade of lieutenant colonel.[4]

The comparison of military and civilian compensation is limited by the fact that military and civilian jobs differ significantly. The military may require a generous retirement system to maintain the young and vigorous force needed for combat. For this reason, the Congressional Budget Office compared the lifetime retirement benefits of a career enlisted man with the benefits provided under a typical but hypothetical system for police and fire fighters—a group for whom the maintenance

---

1   Congressional Budget Office, *The Military Retirement System: Options for Change* (Washington, D.C., January 1978), p. 6.

2   Richard H.L. Cooper, *Military Manpower and the All-Volunteer Force*, R-1450-ARPA (Rand Corporation, September 1977), pp. 364–379.

3   Senate Appropriations Committee, *Report to Accompany H.R. 7933, Department of Defense Appropriation Bill 1978*, S. Rept. 325, Vol. 95, No. 1 (July 1, 1977), pp. 22–28.

4   "Shaping the Defense Civil Work Force," a study prepared for the Senate Committee on Armed Services, *Committee Print*, Vol. 95, No. 1 (September 1977), p. 33.

Table 5-1.   Lifetime Retirement Earnings of a Typical U.S. Enlisted Person under Alternative Formulas (in 1978 dollars)[a]

Retirement Formula	Earnings of Those Who Retire after 20 Years of Service	Earnings of Those Who Retire after 30 Years of Service
U.S. military	190,000	310,000
Typical private	10,000	40,000
Typical nonfederal public	15,000	60,000
Federal civil service[b]	20,000	70,000
Typical police officer/fire fighter	70,000	225,000
Australian military	255,000	320,000
British military	(Not allowed until 22 years of service)	285,000
Canadian military	120,000	245,000
West German military	(Not allowed until age 52)	330,000[c]

[a] These numbers assume a U.S. enlisted person enters the service at age 19, progresses through the system at the median pay grade, earning current U.S. military pay and allowances, and then retires after 20 or 30 years of service under the retirement formulas of either the U.S. military or other systems. Numbers assume price and wage growth of 5 and 6 percent, but costs are deflated to constant 1978 dollars by dividing by cumulative price growth. For simplicity, numbers are not discounted. Discounting at 5 percent, real interest does not change the general conclusions. Specifics underlying these numbers are based primarily on findings of the Defense Manpower Commission and DOD, *The Third Quadrennial Review of Military Compensation* (December 1976).

[b] These lifetime retirement earnings may not reflect earnings of some civil service retirees. A civil service retiree with 30 years of service, who is also age 55, could retire with an immediate annuity. A military enlisted person with 30 years of service is age 49, and so under the civil service formula would not receive benefits until age 62. A similar caveat applies to 20-year retirees.

[c] For illustration, numbers for West Germany assume retirement is allowed at age 49, but the annuity is not assumed to begin until age 52.

Source: Congressional Budget Office, *The Military Retirement System: Options for Change* (Washington, D.C., January 1978), Table 2, p. 20.

of a young and vigorous force would also be important. The comparison revealed that military benefits are more than double those of the typical police or fire plan for enlisted personnel with 20 years of service and about 30 percent higher for employees with 30 years (see Table 5-1). Earlier retirement age, lack of employee contributions and postretirement cost-of-living adjustments all contributed to the higher military lifetime pension benefits.

That the military system is more generous than typical plans available to public civilian workers, private-sector workers, or even police and fire fighters is rarely disputed. The question is whether such high levels of compensation are required to attract the desired workforce. Two pieces of information provide evidence for evaluating this issue. The first is a study the Conference Board prepared for the

Department of Defense which indicated that the military may be paying the appropriate salaries to attract officers with the necessary qualifications.[5] This conclusion was based on a comparison of the distribution of salaries among managers in a sample of seven companies with the distribution of salaries of military officers.[6] The comparison revealed a similar pattern and found that at very senior levels, the military had many fewer high-paid officers. However, the omission of retirement benefits from the study severely limits the usefulness of the comparison.

The second consideration in evaluating the adequacy of military pension benefits is the availability of alternative sources of postretirement income. The typical enlisted person retiring in 1978 will receive about $6,000 in retirement pay while the typical officer will get about $15,000.[7] In addition, at age 62 military retirees are eligible for social security benefits. Between termination of military service and attainment of age 62, most retirees undertake a second career.[8]

A 1975 analysis of the tax returns of military retirees provides an overall picture of retirement earnings.[9] Median-adjusted gross income of these returns fell between $15,000 and $16,000 with only 8 percent below $5,000. While the tax data reveal that few military retirees have very low incomes, another study indicates that military retirees do not earn as much in their second career jobs as comparable civilians.[10] It is unclear whether the lower earnings of second-career military retirees can be attributed to a less marketable background or to occupational or locational choice. Military retirees tend to move to the South where earnings are lower so that geographical discrepancies may account for the differential in earnings between military retirees and nonretirees with similar age and education. These issues will be addressed in a study now being conducted by Rand.

Police and Fire Fighters

Pension plans for police and fire fighters are numerous and vary widely. Although employees in the police and fire category comprise only 6.7 percent of all covered state and local workers, police and fire plans constitute two-thirds of all

---

5   Ruth G. Shaeffer, *Comparative Staffing Patterns, A Special Report for the Department of Defense of Preliminary Research Conducted by the Conference Board* (New York: The Conference Board, 1974).

6   The seven companies were chosen to be as similar as possible to the Department of Defense in size, diversity of mission and other characteristics.

7   CBO, *The Military Retirement System*, p. 22.

8   A 1967 study showed that 95 percent of retirees aged 35 to 54 had second-career civilian jobs. See Alan E. Fletcher and Bette S. Mahoney, "The Economics of Military Retirement," Research Paper P–414, Institute of Defense Analysis (July 1967), p. 9.

9   Senate Appropriations Committee, *Report to Accompany H.R. 7933*, pp. 39–50.

10   U.S. Department of Defense, *Report of the First Quadrennial Review of Military Compensation*, Summary of the Military Estate Program and Vol. IV (January 15, 1969), p. II-9.

state-local plans.[11] Most plans are quite small, including fewer than 200 members.[12] As a group these plans are usually very different from pension plans for other public employees and tend to resemble the retirement plan for military personnel.

While the characteristics of these plans are diverse and complex, it is possible to describe features of what might be considered a "typical" plan. Robert Tilove, in a recent study of state-local retirement systems, surveyed a large number of plans and summarized the following characteristics for a typical police and fire plan.[13]

Benefit formula: an employee's normal pension is equivalent to 50 percent of final pay. Additional benefits are earned at a rate of 1.67 percent for each year of service over the minimum required for a normal benefit.

Retirement age: employees may retire with normal benefits at age 50 or 55 after completing 20 to 25 years of service. Generally, there are no early retirement provisions.

Vesting: rights to a deferred retirement benefit are acquired after 15 years.

Survivor benefits: widows and surviving dependent children are eligible for annuities ranging from 25 to 50 percent of pay if death is not service-connected and up to two-thirds of final pay if service-connected.

Disability benefits: employees are eligible for disability benefits after five years of service. These benefits amount to 33 to 50 percent of salary if disability is not service-connected and up to two-thirds for service-connected disabilities.

Postretirement adjustments: automatic cost-of-living increases are not provided by most plans.

Employee contributions: employees contribute 6 percent of pay to the plan.

Social security coverage: only 36 percent of police and fire fighters are covered by social security.[14]

Two conclusions emerge from the description of the typical benefit plan for police and fire fighters. First, the benefits are more generous and the retirement age earlier than plans for general state and local employees. Second, while these plans have many of the characteristics of the military retirement system, police and fire fighters receive considerably lower pensions than armed-services personnel. The two primary factors are the contributory nature of the plan and the lack of automatic cost-of-living adjustments.

Over the 10 to 15 years between retirement from public employment at age 50 to 55 and attainment of normal retirement age, inflation will significantly erode the value of the police or fire fighter's benefits. Although the retiree has received generous retirement benefits during what are normally considered productive working years, that worker will arrive at age 65 with dramatically reduced purchasing power. Moreover, the absence of productivity adjustments to benefits means that

---

11   U.S. House of Representatives, Committee on Education and Labor, *Pension Task Force Report on Public Employee Retirement Systems*, 95th Cong., 2nd sess., March 15, 1978, p. 57.

12   Robert Tilove, *Public Employee Pension Funds* (New York: Columbia University Press, 1976), p. 222.

13   Ibid., p. 223.

14   *Pension Task Force Report*, Table B–7, p. 59.

the retiree's standard of living will have declined even more drastically relative to that of employees who have worked to age 65. Thus, although retirement benefits for uniformed personnel are far more expensive to provide and initially more generous than those of general employees, they fail to provide the same measure of financial security during normal retirement years when opportunities for supplementing pension income with earnings are severely limited.

While the pensions for police and fire fighters are generous for those who stay long enough to retire, the long vesting period works to the disadvantage of short-service personnel. The problem is particularly serious for these workers because only 36.4 percent of police and fire fighters are covered by social security.[15] They have traditionally opposed social security coverage for fear that it might impinge on their preferential pension provisions and in recognition of their ability to work in covered employment after retirement from protective services. This scheme works to the advantage of those who retire, collect benefits and gain minimum coverage under social security, but exposes those who fail to achieve the 15-year vesting requirements to substantial gaps in protection.

The earlier vesting requirements for disability benefits tend to offset the long vesting period for retirement benefits. Retirement on the basis of service-connected disability is widespread. The police in Washington, D.C. provide an extreme example where three-fourths of beneficiaries retire on service-connected disability. Disability programs appear to be administered very leniently; many state and city plans presume that any heart disability is service-connected.[16]

In summary, total compensation (including pension benefits) for military personnel and police and fire fighters is significantly higher than compensation for civilian workers both inside and outside the government. Greater compensation may be required to induce individuals to assume the arduous tasks, longer hours and risk of bodily injury endemic to protective service jobs. Little direct evidence exists to support the contention that overall compensation is excessive. However, the normal problems of compensation determination in the public sector are exacerbated by the absence of private-sector counterparts for these occupations. Although the existence of shortages or surpluses of applicants for these jobs provides some indication of the adequacy of wages, lack of knowledge about the impact of pensions on career choice prevents drawing conclusions about the entire compensation package. Nevertheless, specific provisions of the pension plans for this group of workers have received considerable criticism, and several proposals for reform have been put forth.

CRITICISM OF PROVISIONS

Criticism of pension plans for the military as well as police and fire fighters has focused on three issues: high costs, early retirement and inadequate provisions for those who fail to satisfy the service requirements. While the costs of military re-

---

15   Ibid. This figure is consistent with that estimated by Tilove. See Tilove, *Public Employee Pension Funds*, p. 233.

16   Tilove, *Public Employee Pension Funds*, p. 239.

tirement pensions have increased dramatically from $1.2 billion in 1964 to $9.1 billion in 1978, high costs alone cannot provide the basis for revising a retirement program for workers who provide essential services. The issue is whether the personnel needs of DOD as well as state and local governments could be met with alternative levels of wages, allowances and retirement benefits. More specifically, the question is whether early retirement, generous annuities and long vesting are the most efficient and equitable mechanisms to achieve the desired personnel profile.

Early Retirement

Early and generous retirement benefits coupled with mandatory retirement provisions at the state-local levels have been defended as necessary to maintain a young and vigorous workforce capable of coping with arduous physical tasks or, in the case of the military, of engaging in combat. By facilitating the dismissal of older personnel, these provisions open up new jobs and increase the advancement potential for younger workers.

In the military, the monetary incentives to complete just 20 years of service and retire are very strong. The typical enlisted person who completes 15 years acquires retirement benefits equivalent to $18,690 in annual pay by staying 5 years more. After 20 years, the value of additional retirement benefits earned by staying another 5 years amounts to only $3,830 per year.[17] With these incentives, it is not surprising that more than 95 percent of all officers and enlisted persons who complete 15 years remain to complete 20 years of service. Just as predictably, only one-fourth of all officers and less than one-tenth of enlisted persons who stay for 20 years go on to complete 25 years of service.

While these losses at 20 years of service are consistent with DOD's stated personnel management objectives, many have criticized the necessity of maintaining such a youthful force. Admiral Hyman Rickover has stated that "there are today few jobs in the military that cannot be performed by persons up to 55 years of age or even older."[18] Furthermore, many career military personnel do not serve in jobs that demand exceptional physical stamina because these positions are usually filled by junior military personnel who leave before retiring. According to the preliminary results of a survey conducted by the General Accounting Office, on average only 8 percent of the enlisted retiree's career has been spent in jobs rated as the most physically demanding, and 80 percent of enlisted retirees never spent any time in positions categorized as most physically demanding.[19] For officers, the percent of

---

17   CBO, *The Military Retirement System*, p. 9.

18   Testimony of Admiral Hyman Rickover before the Subcommittee on Investigations of the Committee on Post Office and Civil Service, U.S. House of Representatives, 95th Cong., 2nd sess. See Hearings Proceedings, *Dual Compensation—Retired Military Personnel in Federal Civilian Positions* (Washington, D.C., 1977), p. 6.

19   Physically demanding jobs include positions in the following categories: infantry, armor and amphibious jobs; artillery; gunnery; rocket and missile areas; combat engineering; combat air crews; and seamanship specialities. The GAO report has not been released; preliminary results were obtained by the CBO. See *The Military Retirement System*, p. 11.

time spent in jobs directly involving technical operations averaged 34 percent of an average retiree's career, while 30 percent spent no time in such jobs.

These results do not, however, provide strong support for elimination of early retirement provisions since most of the military retirees surveyed in the Report for the Senate Committee on Armed Services entered the armed forces during peacetime (around 1955). More importantly, even if career personnel do not routinely serve in physically demanding positions, many of them must be ready to perform these types of jobs in case of war.

Vesting

Long vesting periods have been used to encourage employees to remain in active service and minimize the loss of specially trained personnel. However, these vesting provisions sometimes have been deemed unfair. Those who leave the military with less than 20 years of service—which include more than 90 percent of all enlisted entrants and more than 70 percent of all officer entrants—receive no benefits at all. In contrast, those who complete 20 years earn substantial benefits. The same problem arises at the state and local levels where police and fire fighters must complete 15 years of service before they are eligible for any annuity.

Immediate Annuity

Because most military personnel and members of protective services at the state and local levels undertake second careers, it is not clear that a compelling reason exists for making annuities available immediately upon retirement from public employment. Some suggest education and retraining would be more effective than pension annuities in facilitating transition to a second career. This would permit reorienting the focus of retirement policy toward providing full retirement income at a normal retirement age.

PROPOSALS FOR REFORM

In response to the extensive criticism of the current retirement systems for workers in hazardous employment, numerous studies have been undertaken and many changes recommended. In the last 10 years, six major studies have been done on the military retirement system, and some consensus has emerged on the nature of the required reforms.[20] Although these studies have focused on the military retire-

---

20   DOD, *Report of the First Quadrennial Review of Military Compensation; Report to the President on the Study of Uniformed Services Retirement and Survivor Benefits by the Interagency Committee*, Volume I (July 1, 1971) and Volume II (August 1972); DOD, *Report to the Secretary of Defense by the DOD Retirement Study Group* (May 31, 1972); Defense Manpower Commission, *Defense Manpower: The Keystone of National Security*, Report to the President and the Congress (along with Volume V of the staff studies), (April 1976); DOD, *The Third Quadrennial Review of Military Compensation*, History and Volume III and Volume IX of the staff studies (December 1976); *Report of the President's Commission on Military Compensation* (April 1978).

ment system, many of the recommendations are applicable to plans for police and fire fighters.

Reduced Annuities before 30 Years

All the major studies propose reducing annuities for those who retire before 30 years of service. Such a reduction would both lower costs and encourage trained personnel to remain for more than 20 years. The exact nature of the proposed reduction varies considerably depending on the study.

A proposal drafted by a DOD study group and introduced in Congress in 1974, 1975 and 1976 would reduce the current annuity available after 20 years of service by 30 percent, restoring the full value after 30 years of service. For example, the typical enlisted person retiring at age 39 with 20 years of service currently receives an immediate lifetime annuity of $5,800. Under the proposed scheme, the benefit available after 20 years would be reduced to $4,010 (reflecting the 30 percent reduction). Between 20 and 30 years of service, the benefit would be gradually increased to its full amount so that a retiree with 30 years of service would receive approximately the $5,800. When the retiree's social security payments begin at age 65 (or age 62), the military annuity under this option would drop to reflect the social security offset.

This proposal involves only modest changes in the retirement program and therefore would have only a modest impact on costs and the pattern of military careers. Savings would amount to about $1 billion per year (in 1978 dollars) by the year 2000 with a total of $11 billion between now and the end of the century. In terms of the personnel profile, the reduced annuity for 20 years would lessen the incentive to complete 20 years of service, but the rising annuity after 20 years would encourage careerists to remain until 30 years.

A slightly more ambitious scheme was designed by an interagency committee in 1971. Under this plan, annuities are reduced until the retiree reaches a normal retirement age. For a retiree with 20 years of service, the reduction would be 2 percent times the difference between the individual's age at retirement and age 60. For retirees with 25 or more years of service, the reduction would be calculated on the basis of a normal retirement age of 55. When the beneficiary reached the specified normal retirement age, the full accrued benefit would become payable until social security benefits were drawn at age 65 (or 62). At that time, retired pay would be offset against the social security award. For instance, a typical enlisted person retiring at age 39 with 20 years would receive an annuity of $3,364—42 percent less than the current annuity of $5,800. At age 60, the annuity would revert to the $5,800 until age 65 when it would be reduced to $4,000, reflecting the social security offset.

The cost savings under this plan are twice as high—$2 billion annually—as under the 30 percent reduction scheme, and the change would have a greater impact on career patterns. The incentive to stay for 20 years and the push to leave immediately after 20 years would be reduced more than under the 30 percent scheme. A major advantage of this plan is that it is designed to reduce retirement pay during the years when the retiree is likely to hold a civilian job.

The most dramatic proposal is to adopt age eligibility rules for a retirement annuity similar to those in effect for civil servants. Those completing 5 to 19 years of service would receive an annuity beginning at age 62. Those completing 20 to 29 years of service would receive an annuity beginning at age 60, while those completing 30 or more years would receive an annuity at age 55. However, this plan differs significantly from the federal civil service system. In both the civilian and the proposed military plans, workers with the necessary years of service who retire prior to the stipulated retirement age receive deferred annuities. However, under the proposed scheme, the annuity would be indexed for inflation between termination and the time the individual attains retirement age. This would insulate young retirees from erosion of deferred pension benefits due to use of an absolute compensation base in the benefits calculation.

Other important differences from the civil service plan are the noncontributory nature of the military plan and a generous severance-pay feature. Persons involuntarily separated with less than 30 years of service would be entitled to a substantial cash bonus (equal to one year's pay for those retiring with 20 years). This option would substantially modify the entire pattern of military careers. Fewer personnel would tend to complete 20 years, but many more of those with 20 years would probably stay for careers of 30 years or more.

This final scheme has considerable applicability for police and fire fighters. While compelling reasons exist for allowing workers engaged in an arduous occupation such as fire fighting to retire from that occupation at a reasonably young age with a secure benefit, retirement does not necessarily require the immediate payment of an annuity. Most fire fighters and police move on to second careers. Generous severance pay could be provided to facilitate the transition to a new job as suggested by the President's Commission on Military Compensation.[21] However, the annuity could be postponed to a normal retirement age with indexing for inflation to prevent the erosion of the value of benefits.

Earlier Vesting

Long vesting periods have been used to encourage continuous employment and minimize the loss of specially trained personnel. However, five of the six studies on military compensation mentioned earlier have recommended vesting in the military for persons with less than 20 years of service.[22] This step would eliminate the serious inequity of denying any benefits to persons who leave after 19 years while providing generous pensions to those who complete 20 years of service. At the state-local levels, earlier vesting would provide much needed protection to short-service police and fire employees who generally are not covered under social security. Vesting would also increase management flexibility by allowing managers to sever unneeded personnel without depriving them of future pensions.

---

21   *Report of the President's Commission on Military Compensation*, p. 70.

22   The exception is the 1969 *Report to the First Quadrennial Review of Military Compensation*.

Considerable consensus was found among the military studies on when and how much vesting should occur. All the studies in favor of earlier vesting recommended that some benefits should be provided to persons who leave voluntarily with 10 or more years of service. This would make the military plan consistent with the vesting standards established for private plans under ERISA. Most of the studies also recommended that those leaving voluntarily receive a deferred annuity, beginning at age 60 or 65, rather than a lump-sum payment, and that benefits be extended to personnel who leave involuntarily after 5 or more years of service.

Employee Contributions

The military system is one of the few public pension plans that does not require employees to contribute to their retirement benefits. Five of the six studies recommended that the system remain noncontributory.[23] However, there is considerable support in Congress for making the system contributory. If instituting employee contributions did not require offsetting pay raises, such a system would save the government money. Employee participation might also make military personnel aware of the costs of their benefits. However, most studies concluded that the disadvantages outweigh the gains from introducing contributions at this stage. In the absence of an offsetting pay raise, contributions would be equivalent to a salary cut for military personnel and might make it more difficult to attract qualified people. Furthermore, the potential of a refund of contributions might encourage military personnel to leave after their first enlistment.

In summary, numerous studies of the military system have been conducted, and a large variety of proposals has been made to adopt reforms. Some of the proposals could also be applied to plans for police and fire fighters—particularly the concept of a deferred annuity with substantial severance pay to help in the transition to a new career.

Higher Wages

One type of proposal not widely considered is changing the mix of salaries and pension benefits. Providing higher pay instead of generous pensions would make it possible to attract the desired workers for the truly hazardous occupations within an agency. The military already uses some types of incentive pay for particularly hazardous duty. Additional pay is also available for specific jobs such as parachute jumping, demolition, submarine, and flight duty. Higher wages would more directly target compensation to the needs of the younger workers the military is eager to attract and would make comparisons of compensation easier for those considering public versus private employment. In short, the retirement systems for workers in hazardous employment must be reformed in the context of the total compensation package required to attract qualified workers.

---

23   Again, the exception is the 1969 *Report of the First Quadrennial Review of Military Compensation*.

SUMMARY

Workers in hazardous employment at both the federal and state-local levels receive generous compensation—especially when the value of pension benefits is considered. The exception is military personnel with less than 20 years of service, who receive no pension. Unfortunately, little evidence exists to determine whether these benefits are required to attract qualified personnel. However, the pensions seem poorly designed in view of the employment patterns of retired personnel. Many military personnel, police officers and fire fighters engage in a second career from which they receive some earnings in years following their retirement from their first job. Should this employment pattern prove to be typical, then a large lump-sum payment—perhaps in combination with education entitlement—to ease the move to a new job may be more appropriate than a lifetime annuity beginning at age 40 or 50. Deferred pension benefits commencing at a normal retirement age would reduce costs and eliminate salary-annuity dipping (described in Chapter 4).

6

Public Employee Plans and Social Security

When social security was originally enacted in 1935, many categories of workers, among them public employees, were excluded from the program. Federal employees were omitted because the majority were already protected under the federal civil service retirement system. Although most state and local workers were not similarly covered by employer-sponsored plans, they were excluded because it has been assumed that the Constitution legally prevented the federal government from imposing a tax on states and municipalities. However, as social security coverage was expanded to include virtually all private-sector employees, coverage was also broadened to include many public workers. In 1950, coverage was offered to some state and local workers. State and city employers could elect to join social security (making the taxation voluntary) if their workers were not already participating in another retirement system. Subsequent Amendments to the Social Security Act further broadened public employee coverage to include the armed forces (1956)[1] and state-local employees already under pension plans if both they and their employers chose to participate (1954).[2]

As a result of repeated coverage extensions, most public employees now participate in the social security program. There are, however, important exceptions. Members of the federal civil service as well as 30 percent of state and local employees represent a significant group still remaining outside the system. The exclusion of these public workers has generated two types of serious problems. First, the present system is inequitable since those workers who are entitled to pensions sponsored by nonparticipating government employers can gain minimum coverage under social security and profit from the benefit structure, which was designed to help low-wage workers rather than workers whose second career entitled them to benefits. Second, employees lacking social security coverage are exposed to a variety of gaps in basic protection—most notably in the areas of survivor, disability and postretirement medical insurance.

AREAS OF OVERLAP

The absence of any coordination between the excluded public plans and social

---

1 Prior to 1957, members of the armed forces had been granted gratuitous wage credits for services rendered since the start of World War II. Only in 1956 was normal compulsory coverage applied to the military, however.

2 Fire fighters and police were excluded until 1956 when five states were permitted to elect coverage for those categories of workers. Subsequently, the provision was expanded to apply to police and fire fighters in 21 states and Puerto Rico. In addition, fire fighters in other states can be provided with coverage at the state's option provided the governor certifies that the extension of coverage will improve the overall protection of the fire fighters.

security has created a significant potential for benefit overlap. Public employees without regular social security coverage and eligible for early retirement, such as federal civil servants, police and fire fighters, can easily gain social security protection as a result of a second career. Dual beneficiaries of social security and pensions sponsored by excluded employers are in a position to benefit from weighting in the social security benefit formula designed for low-wage earners. Under social security, workers with low lifetime earnings are protected against an inadequate retirement income by a steeply progressive benefit formula and a minimum benefit provision which ensure such workers a heavily subsidized return on their contributions. However, since a worker's monthly earnings are calculated by averaging covered earnings over a typical working lifetime rather than over the actual years of covered employment,[3] a high-wage earner with a short period of time in covered employment cannot be distinguished from an individual who worked a lifetime in covered employment at exceptionally low wages. Therefore, a worker who is entitled to a civil service or state or local pension and achieves insured status under social security through "moonlighting" or a second career can qualify for heavily subsidized benefits.[4]

A high incidence of dual beneficiaries among federal civil service retirees has been documented by both the Social Security Administration and the federal Civil Service Commission. In 1975, 31 percent of civil service retirees with 30 years of service and 73 percent with 12 to 29 years of service received OASDHI benefits.[5] About 28 percent of all civil service annuitants receiving social security benefits had earned the minimum benefit (compared to 14 percent for the population as a whole), and roughly 75 percent had average monthly earnings below the median, thereby entitling them to subsidized benefits (see Table 6–1). Although less is known about the incidence of dual beneficiaries among employees of nonparticipating state and local governments, it is likely that a significant proportion of these annuitants are dual beneficiaries.[6]

---

3   The average monthly earnings computation period is the number of years after 1950 (or age 21) to the age of 62 less five years of lowest earnings. Thus, in 1978 the computation period for a worker retiring at age 65 is 19 years. The period will lengthen by one year every year until 1994, at which point it will stabilize at 35 years.

4   Minimum covered employment required to be fully insured under social security is 1 quarter of covered employment for each year after 1950 (or age 21) measured to age 62 with a minimum of 6 quarters and a maximum of 40 quarters. Thus, for all new employees the requirement is 10 years of service in covered employment.

5   See Daniel N. Price and Andrea Novotny, "Federal Civil Service Annuitants and Social Security, December, 1975," Social Security Bulletin, Vol. 40 (November 1977), pp. 3–18. The findings of this study are consistent with the results of an earlier federal Civil Service Commission report which indicated that 4 out of 10 civil service annuitants also received OASDHI benefits. See federal Civil Service Commission, The 1972 Survey of Income of Civil Service Annuitants (Washington, D.C., 1973).

6   Another group of dual beneficiaries has been able to collect social security without working even a minimal period in covered employment. In 1975, 5 percent of federal civil service annuitants who were ineligible for social security on the basis of their own earnings collected benefits based on the earnings records of their eligible spouses. However, legislation in December 1977 corrected this inequity by requiring an offset of pension income from uncovered employment against the spouse's benefit for future public-sector annuitants.

Table 6–1.   Comparison of Distributions of Civil Service Annuitants
and All Social Security Retirees by Social Security
Primary Insurance Amount, 1975

PIA	Civil Service Annuitants	All Social Security Retirees
$101.40	27.8%	13.8%
101.50–129.90	13.5	6.4
130.00–159.90	17.5	10.7
160.00–189.90	12.4	11.6
190.00–249.90	15.5	20.8
250.00–299.00	8.8	22.8
300 or more	4.5	13.8
Total	100.0	100.0

Sources: Daniel N. Price and Andrea Novotny, "Federal Civil Service Annuitants
and Social Security, 1975," *Social Security Bulletin*, Vol. 40 (November 1977), Table
9, p. 14; and unpublished data from the Social Security Administration, Office of
Research and Statistics.

Also, gains to dual beneficiaries raise the cost of social security for all other
participants. Lifetime members support a higher payroll tax (about 0.35 percent of
covered payrolls) in order to provide a welfare subsidy to retirees who have enjoyed
an adequate income throughout their working lives and who already have the security of another government pension. The return to lifetime members is thus
depressed by the amount of the subsidy implicit in the returns to double dippers.
The wide divergence in returns available to workers with identical earnings histories,
because of a difference in the coverage status of their primary employment, is a
serious horizontal inequity.

Furthermore, excluded workers bear none of the responsibility for meeting the
basic needs of the nation's poor elderly and disabled. To the extent that the social
security program is redistributive, high-wage government workers who do not participate escape this burden of support. Viewed in these terms, exemption from
social security is equivalent to one of the many types of tax privileges available to
high-wage earners. Inclusion of these workers would result in a more equitable
distribution of the welfare burden and would reduce the cost to other participants.[7]

GAPS IN PROTECTION

While the lack of universal coverage enables some public employees to profit from
the progressive benefit formula, other public workers are exposed to serious gaps

7   Recent Social Security Administration estimates indicate that if all public employees were brought
into the system there would be a long-term reduction in cost of OASDHI of 0.33 percent of covered
wages and a short-term reduction of 0.70 percent.

in protection. An estimated 2.4 percent of full-time government workers are not insured by either an independent pension plan or social security and therefore are completely unprotected.[8] Even workers who are under a government plan may lack some basic protection if they are not covered by social security. State and local plans vary widely in the scope and level of benefits as well as in the stringency of vesting provisions required for eligibility. Although federal plans are more consistent, they too fail to provide the breadth of protection available under social security.

Government pensions were originally oriented toward the objectives of supporting management needs and increasing the efficiency of the workforce. They emphasize benefits that will (1) help maintain a competitive employment position; (2) induce workers to remain with the organization through the peak of their productivity; (3) keep appointment and promotion opportunities open; and (4) ease adjustments in the size or composition of the workforce as needed to fulfill organizational objectives. Government retirement systems continue to place main emphasis on the retirement benefits and protection of long-service employees.

While retirement benefits for long-service employees under noncovered government plans tend to be more generous than those provided by social security, short-service employees generally are not treated as well as they would be under social security. Many police and fire plans do not provide any retirement benefits to workers who terminate with less than 20 years of service. Although most civilian public plans have vesting requirements of about 10 years, mobile workers with less than this amount of service must forfeit all rights to earned pension credits. Unless these workers have been simultaneously covered by social security, they are completely unprotected. Moreover, since employer-sponsored plans usually have strictly wage-related benefit formulas, low-wage government workers receive no special subsidies to retirement income. Finally, workers covered by state and local pensions which do not provide full cost-of-living increases are exposed to the risk of declining real benefits in the face of high rates of inflation.

In addition to a difference in retirement benefits, excluded government workers are exposed to various gaps in postretirement medical insurance and survivorship and disability protection. Employer-sponsored plans are often oriented toward providing a variety of medical benefits suited to the needs of younger current employees and may be less well suited to the health needs of elderly retirees. In contrast, Medicare benefits provide some coverage for extended care in skilled nursing facilities and similar services most frequently required by the aged. Since employer-sponsored plans cannot afford to meet the special needs of both young and old, uncovered retirees usually lack adequate prepaid medical insurance.

Although most government plans provide some form of disability and survivor coverage, the eligibility requirements coupled with the nonportability of benefit rights endanger the protection of mobile workers. Eligibility requirements for disability generally exclude workers with less than 5 to 10 years of service. Although survivor benefits usually require shorter eligibility periods, the benefit to the survivor of a short-service employee is likely to be minimal.

---

8   U.S. House of Representatives, Committee on Education and Labor, *Pension Task Force Report on Public Employee Retirement Systems*, 85th Cong., 2nd sess., March 15, 1978.

Unlike social security rights, entitlements to public pensions are largely non-portable: protection is terminated if the employee leaves prior to retirement. Although federal credits are portable between civil service and most independent federal staff plans, they are inapplicable to any other employment. Likewise, state and local portability is almost always limited to public employment within the same state,[9] and where state and local systems are unconsolidated, disability and survivorship rights may be restricted to employment within a single government agency. Lack of portability means mobile workers are unprotected until social security or subsequent plan vesting requirements are satisfied.

Workers shifting from covered to uncovered employment forfeit social security disability protection after 5¼ years and may eventually lose survivorship protection. Should the eligibility provisions for the excluded employer's plan exceed the relevant time limits, the worker would be without protection in event of death or disability.

ALTERNATIVE APPROACHES TO COORDINATING SOCIAL SECURITY WITH GOVERNMENT PLANS

The exclusion of civil servants and a third of state-local workers from social security leaves some workers without adequate protection. This problem could be reduced or eliminated by changes in the social security benefit calculation, but only universal coverage would ensure all public employees adequate protection for disability, retirement and health.

Modifying the Benefit Calculation

If social security benefits were strictly wage- and service-related, dual beneficiaries would create no problem. Retirees who had participated marginally in the system would receive small benefits based on their minimal contributions. Alternatives to universal coverage, therefore, focus on modifying the social security system to reduce its redistributive components.

The Minimum Benefit.   The high incidence of dual beneficiaries among those eligible for the minimum benefit has cast doubt on whether its stated welfare objective is applicable in this instance. There is evidence that a large portion of minimum benefits is paid to those who are not primarily dependent on earnings in covered employment during their working years and are not primarily dependent on social security benefits during their retirement years. In 1978, minimum benefits were awarded on the basis of average monthly earnings of $76 or less. Earnings of this level suggest very weak attachment to the employment covered by social security since a worker retiring at age 65 in January 1978 who had worked a full career at the prevailing minimum wage would have average monthly earnings of $240.

In order to eliminate the gains to dual beneficiaries, the 1977 Amendments to the Social Security Act froze the regular minimum benefit at $121.80 (subject to

---

9   Teachers have achieved limited interstate portability. See Chapter 4 for a more detailed discussion of portability.

postretirement cost-of-living increases). However, the "special" minimum benefit has been increased to protect long-service low-wage workers. This benefit is calculated by multiplying years of coverage (in excess of 10 but less than 30) by $11.50, an amount which will increase automatically with the consumer price index. The effect is to limit benefits to short-service employees while still protecting long-service low-wage workers.

Freezing the minimum benefit, however, is only a partial solution since dual beneficiaries will continue to profit from the implicit subsidy of the progressive benefit formula.

A Proportional Benefit Formula. An alternative to such partial solutions is a comprehensive overhaul of the social security benefit structure. Introduction of a proportional benefit formula accompanied by the elimination of minimum and dependents' benefits would entirely relieve social security of its redistributive components. Benefits would be calculated as a flat percentage (for example, 40 percent) of workers' average lifetime covered monthly earnings. All participants would receive the same return on contributions because taxes are also calculated as a flat percentage of covered earnings. The welfare function ascribed to social security would be transferred to an expanded Supplemental Security Income (SSI) program in order to ensure low-wage workers an adequate income in retirement.

Such a comprehensive change would eliminate the overlaps existing between social security and pensions sponsored by excluded government employees. However, it fails to address the problem of gaps in protection which the lack of coordination between programs poses.

More fundamentally, introduction of strictly wage-related benefits represents a major redefinition of the role of social security. Although consideration of a broader range of financial and distributional issues may suggest shifting the program to focus more clearly on individual equity, it is difficult to defend such a major redesign on the basis of coordination difficulties with a few government plans. In addition to protecting the interest of excluded employees, it would be far less disruptive to extend coverage to those six million public workers than to modify a system affecting 90 percent of the workforce.

UNIVERSAL COVERAGE

While modifying the social security benefit calculation for public employees would reduce the windfall to dual beneficiaries with minimum coverage, only universal coverage of all public employees under social security can simultaneously assure workers who move in and out of public employment the continuous protection now available to workers in the private sector.

Civil Service

Extending coverage to federal civilian employees would not involve any insurmountable constitutional or administrative problems. However, unions and other organizations of federal workers are strongly opposed to mandatory coverage. To gain support for social security coverage, it would be necessary to devise an integrated benefit structure which ensured that the combined social security and civil service protection was equivalent to the benefits currently provided by the civil service system. Although designing an integrated system is complex, examples of public plans which have been coordinated with social security exist. The Tennessee Valley Authority and railroad retirement plans are two such systems administered at the federal level.

Tennessee Valley Authority Plan.   The TVA retirement system was established in 1939 as a federal staff plan independent of the civil service retirement system. Provisions of the TVA plan were originally more generous to short-service employees than those of civil service since most TVA workers were drawn from private enterprise and in many instances returned there. Mainly because of the discontinuous public employment patterns of its employees, TVA began seeking social security coverage in 1946. In 1950, social security coverage was extended to hourly laborers not eligible under the TVA plan. In 1956, social security coverage was granted to all TVA employees, and an integration plan was devised to coordinate the two retirement systems.

The TVA integration scheme is essentially an offset plan. The retirement benefit is composed of two parts: an annuity based on the employee's contributions and age at retirement and a pension financed by employer contributions. The employer pension is equal to 1.3 percent of the employee's high three-year average salary multiplied by years of service and is reduced by a social security offset. The offset is equal to 2 percent of the employee's social security benefit at age 65, not in excess of $1,050, multiplied by the years of creditable service (not in excess of 30, exclusive of any unused sick leave credit) rendered after December 31, 1955. The effect of the plan is to ensure all workers an equitable return on their own contributions while limiting the employer-sponsored basic protection to prevent duplication of the social security guarantee.

Railroad Retirement System.   In 1935, Congress passed legislation consolidating the efforts of the many fragmented and financially weak employer and union plans then covering railroad workers. Although railroad workers were not originally included under social security,[10] subsequent Amendments to the Railroad Retirement Act modeled benefit provisions after OASDHI arrangements and established an intricate web of financing and benefit coordination provisions between the two systems. As a result of the Railroad Retirement Act of 1974, these complex arrangements were simplified to provide better coordination between the two plans.

Under the Railroad Retirement Act of 1974, railroad workers receive a two-tier benefit. The first tier, computed under the social security benefit formula, is based on the employee's combined railroad and social security service. However, any actual social security benefit the employee is entitled to as a result of work in covered employment is subtracted from that amount, thus preventing a dual payment for the same employment. The second tier, based on only railroad service and earnings, is the sum of several components, each of which reflects the different methods of treating service before and after January 1, 1975, the changeover date established by the Act.

---

10   In fact, the Social Security Act was enacted two weeks before the Railroad Retirement Act of 1935, so that railroad workers were covered under the initial old-age benefits program for this brief period.

In addition, to protect beneficiaries who are eligible for dual benefits on the basis of service before 1975, a special benefit is paid. This payment represents the amount by which the sum of benefits arrived at by calculating benefits *separately* for railroad service and for social security credits exceeds the benefits that accrue as a result of the combined earnings. As a result of the 1974 Amendments, the railroad retirement system is now basically well coordinated with social security and provides an adequate level of benefits in an equitable manner.

Transitional Provisions.   As indicated in both the TVA and railroad retirement schemes, special provisions must usually accompany integration efforts to protect current workers from loss of benefits on which they have based their retirement plans. Usually, three implication schemes are considered during the integration transition. The first of these is exemplified by the TVA plan.

Under the TVA plan, workers are permitted to retain vested benefits earned prior to the 1956 consolidation. Social security was made applicable to service beginning after 1955 except for workers who chose not to join because they were too close to retirement to gain eligibility under OASDHI. Immediate coverage was thereby provided for many workers, although gaps remained temporarily for current short-term employees. Although dual benefits were eliminated for new or short-service employees, long-service workers were still eligible to collect. As a result, the full financial impact of integration was not immediately available to social security.

Retroactive coverage would eliminate all protection gaps and prevent any special gains to dual beneficiaries. Under this approach, the consolidated public plan would reimburse social security for the contributions and interest which would have been paid had the employees been covered over their entire career in government service. In return, retroactive wage credits would be provided all the new participants. This approach, however, is very expensive for the entering government agency and its employees. Moreover, considerable resistance could be expected from older workers who had incorporated their expected windfall gains in their retirement plans.

At the other extreme, social security coverage could be limited to new entrants. This method, however, neither closes coverage gaps for existing employees nor eliminates dual beneficiary problems posed by the current group of workers. The transition will be even longer than under the TVA plan and will require continued administration of the present retirement system as well as the redesigned plan for many years to come.

Whatever method is chosen, transition to integration is a difficult process. However, it is far less cumbersome to modify a newly incorporated staff plan than to redesign the larger social security system to eliminate the problems created by the existence of excluded independent plans.

An Alternative Approach.   As the next best option to full coverage, Robert Ball has suggested a scheme which retains the separation between social security and federal civilian plans but introduces a credit exchange between them.[11] Under this proposal, a worker who is eligible for civil service retirement benefits would have

---

11   See Robert M. Ball, *Social Security—Today and Tomorrow* (New York: Columbia University Press, 1978), p. 202.

social security earnings count toward extra civil service benefits rather than receiving any social security benefits. Conversely, a federal worker who was not eligible for civil service benefits would receive social security based upon that employee's combined federal and social security earnings.

This plan would replace the option of a lump-sum return of civil service contributions to workers who leave government before retirement with the lump-sum return of the difference between social security contributions that would have been paid if the employer were covered by social security and the civil service contributions that were paid. The government would use the savings resulting from this revision to help finance the exchange of credit plan. The Ball proposal would both ensure coverage for workers who change jobs as well as eliminate dual beneficiaries.

State and Local

The issue of state and local employee participation surfaced as a potentially important problem in March 1976 when New York City gave notice that it intended to withdraw 112,000 of the city's municipal workers from the social security program. Surprisingly, the Social Security Act gives public employers the unilateral power to terminate their employees' coverage, whereas state and local coverage under social security is subject to employee referendum.[12] Widespread withdrawal of state and local systems would significantly aggravate the short-run financial difficulties of the social security system since revenues would decline with no immediate reduction in benefit liability.

Financial pressures prompted New York City's move to withdraw. States and municipalities faced with rising costs and limited potential for tax increases have looked upon withdrawal and elimination of the payroll tax burden as the source of much needed fiscal relief. Studies done for several major plans indicate that the potential for savings is illusory once the cost of substituting the extensive protection lost through termination of social security is considered.[13] There are essentially three reasons why it is so costly for state and local governments to replace social security benefits: actuarial and administrative inefficiency, tax-exempt status of social security benefits, and cost-of-living adjustments to benefits.

Implementing a plan to replace social security benefits would require the addition of administrative staff to oversee the program. An inverse relationship exists between the size of the plan and the percentage of revenues devoted to such administrative expenses. Independent plans, unable to duplicate the efficiencies of scale available to a large program like social security, must expend a larger percentage of payroll in order to provide the same protection provided under OASDHI.

Unlike social security, public pension benefits are subject to federal taxation which reduces the disposable income available to the retirees. Benefits provided under independent plans must therefore be larger in dollar amount to provide

---

12   For an excellent discussion of the coverage provisions under social security, see Robert W. Kalman and Michael T. Leibig, *The Public Pension Crisis: Myth, Reality, Reform*, draft (March 1978).

13   Studies done for the city of New York, the state of Alaska and the state of California all recommended against withdrawal because of the prohibitive cost of replacing lost social security benefits.

Table 6-2.   Estimated Cost of Alternative Social Security Replacement Programs for Alaska State Employees

Alternative	Cost as Percent of Payroll	
(1) Full replacement of social security benefits	22.21	
	Immediate Eligibility for Ancillary Benefits	5-Year Eligibility for Ancillary Benefits[*]
(2) Full benefits	19.25	15.48
(3) Same as #2 above, but cost-of-living adjustment restricted to 3 percent per year	17.87	14.47
(4) Same as #2 above, but no family benefit	15.47	12.50

*Ancillary benefits refer to social security disability and death benefits. It is assumed, under Alternatives 2, 3 and 4, that these ancillary benefits are only available to workers while employed by the state. Upon termination of employment, these benefits will no longer be in effect.

Source: William M. Mercer, *State of Alaska: Factors in Consideration of Termination from the Social Security System*, June 1, 1976, in Robert W. Kalman and Michael T. Leibig, *The Public Pension Crisis: Myth, Reality, Reform*, draft (March 1978).

retirees the same consumption value as social security. This shift in tax status further increases the cost to government agencies seeking to replace fully social security protection.

Even if the initial value of benefits is equivalent to social security, the state must provide expensive cost-of-living adjustments if purchasing power is to be maintained. This fact is often overlooked since many state and local plans currently do not adjust pension benefits for price increases. Only a few of those that do index provide full inflation compensation. The cost of inflation adjustments will also be higher for independent plans because percentage increases will be applicable to a higher pretax benefit. Table 6-2 provides an example of the higher cost of providing equivalent benefits through an independent plan.

The high cost of replacing social security benefits implies that many government agencies which withdraw from the system will not be able to duplicate lost protection. However, even if equivalent benefits were provided, many workers would be adversely affected by withdrawal. Young workers not yet vested under social security would have to forfeit their accumulated payroll tax contributions unless they were able to achieve social security entitlement through subsequent covered employment. Perhaps more significantly, the loss of fully portable wage credits would expose workers to the gaps in protection which noncovered workers face in moving between covered and uncovered employment.

Some groups of workers favor withdrawal, however. Older workers already vested under social security and workers who are eligible to collect spouses' benefits would benefit from dual beneficiary windfall gains as a result of termination. Such workers are gambling that corrective action to eliminate double dipping will not be taken until after their retirement.

New York City's subsequent decision to remain within social security reflects its concern over the real costs of withdrawal. From social security's perspective, the withdrawal of large public systems is also costly since termination immediately cuts off payroll tax revenues but does not cancel the obligation to pay benefits to vested employees.

Mandatory coverage of all state and local workers, however, is a difficult issue because of the constitutional question of whether the federal government has the right to levy a tax on a state or local government. The conflicting legal arguments will ultimately have to be resolved in the courts. If the courts ruled against direct taxation of state and local governments, perhaps the federal government could tie revenue-sharing funds or some other type of federal aid to coverage of all state and local workers under the social security system. Another alternative would be to levy the tax only on state and local workers and then award them only one-half the benefits available to other workers. This scheme might create significant political pressure from public employees for state and local governments to contribute. However, if awarding partial benefits were judged undesirable, full benefits could be provided with the employer's portion of the tax financed through general revenues. As a last resort, a possible option is to extend compulsory coverage directly to the workers and tax them at the self-employed rate, thereby avoiding a tax on state and local governments. The tax treatment of ministers and American citizens employed by international agencies or foreign governments provides a well-established precedent for such a move. However, a higher tax on public than on private workers seems quite unfair. Moreover, none of these alternative schemes may be necessary if the courts were to rule that taxation of state and local governments was permissible.

SUMMARY

The majority of public employees receive social security coverage in addition to the protection provided by employer-sponsored pension plans. However, the exclusion from social security of federal civil servants and 30 percent of state and local workers has generated a number of serious problems.

Employees lacking social security coverage are exposed to a variety of gaps in basic protection—most notably in the areas of survivor, disability and post-retirement medical insurance. Such workers can earn rights to some of the benefits provided by social security by working a minimal period of time in covered employment. However, due to the design of the social security program, workers who achieve eligibility through short service in covered employment benefit from welfare subsidies intended for low-income workers.

Although redesign of the social security program would eliminate the gains accruing to dual beneficiaries of OASDHI and excluded pensions, such a solution would not close the breaches in basic protection which noncovered workers experience. Inclusion of those currently outside the system would both correct the inequity of double dipping and ensure that all workers are afforded the same level of basic insurance.

Universal coverage would, however, force currently excluded employers to alter certain of their pension provisions. Integration schemes would have to be devised to prevent loss of accrued benefits as well as to ensure that retirees do not receive excessively high replacement rates. Transition devices such as those employed by the TVA or railroad retirement plans would also be necessary to protect workers unable to adjust their retirement plans from extraordinary losses when benefit formulas are changed.

The momentum for extension of universal coverage has suffered some setbacks recently. Since 1976, several state and local systems have filed notice of their intentions to withdraw from the system. The withdrawal movement has been motivated in large measure by employers' hopes of fiscal relief from the immediate elimination of the social security payroll tax. However, recognition of the high cost associated with providing benefits equivalent to those of OASDHI has convinced at least New York City to reconsider and retract its notice. This may mark a reversal of the withdrawal movement.

Rectification of the problems created by exclusion of some public workers from social security will involve difficult adjustments regardless of what solution is chosen. However, the problem is serious and attention should be devoted to correcting it.

7

Issues, Options and Further Study

Since public pension plans have developed within the political arena, it is not surprising they have evolved in a haphazard fashion. Under the current array of federal, state and local systems, some public employees are exposed to gaps in coverage while others enjoy relatively generous or multiple benefits. Although the inequities and overlaps have persisted for some time, the rising costs of all public pensions now require that the present system be reevaluated in order to develop a consistent retirement policy.

The previous chapters have surveyed the major issues concerning public-employee pension plans. On the basis of this survey, this chapter will highlight the most crucial problems, note some of the alternative proposals which have been suggested for corrective action, and identify those areas where further research is required. The lists of problems, policy options and areas for further study are not intended to be comprehensive, but rather to illustrate the range of possible reforms. Moreover, while the analysis focuses primarily on economic considerations, clearly the future of public pensions in the context of a national retirement policy has significantly broader social implications.

THE LEVEL OF PUBLIC PENSION BENEFITS

While wages and salaries of public employees are roughly equivalent to those provided private workers, pension benefits are often more favorable. The advantage stems not so much from the initial replacement rate, which often does not exceed the level of private plans when the value of employee contributions is taken into account, but rather from earlier retirement ages and postretirement cost-of-living adjustments.

While exceptions exist, the annuities provided by government plans generally replace a reasonable portion of preretirement earnings. The guidelines established in Chapter 2 indicated that retirees require 65 to 80 percent of previous earnings to maintain their preretirement levels of consumption. Public pension benefits alone rarely exceed the upper bound. However, in those cases where public employees are also entitled to social security and the plans are not integrated, the combined replacement rate may be excessive.

The provision of postretirement cost-of-living adjustments is a rational mechanism to protect retirees from the vagaries of economic performance. If the original benefit is set at a level that is sufficient to maintain preretirement living standards, high rates of inflation should not be allowed to erode the economic welfare of the pensioner. Concern that cost-of-living adjustments have an inflationary impact on the economy as a whole is unwarranted. These adjustments compensate for past changes in prices and differ dramatically in terms of their effect on inflation from wage settlements which include anticipated price increases in negotiated contracts. To the extent that cost-of-living increases simply represent higher total benefits, they do require higher payroll taxes which clearly add to business costs. On the other hand, if these benefits were not provided by social security, then private pensions would be required to play a larger role which would also increase business costs. Indexed social security benefits might contribute indirectly to inflation by insulating a large segment of the population, thereby reducing the size of the constituency resistant to price increases. However, this phenomenon does not represent a strong argument for limiting cost-of-living adjustments in an inflationary environment.

However, the total value of the annuities provided by public plans depends on not only the level of benefits, but also the duration of benefit payments. Federal civilian and military pensions as well as state and local plans for police and fire fighters permit retirement at age 55 or lower. This retirement age is clearly out of line with the national standard of 62 to 65 as defined by the social security program and applied in the private sector. Furthermore, in light of demographic developments and the improved health and life expectancy of the elderly, encouraging early retirement through lowered retirement ages seems questionable.

Options

The high costs of public pension benefits have become increasingly visible, generating concern and resentment among taxpayers who do not enjoy similar protection. The following illustrate some avenues for cost reduction.

Option 1: Reduce public pension benefits by increasing the retirement age to that prevailing in the private sector.

Option 2: Reduce benefits by decreasing replacement rates and extending the retirement age, but maintain cost-of-living adjustments.

Option 3: Extend the existing comparability standards for wages to include fringe benefits.[1]

Information

Considerable information already exists which can be used to select the appropriate avenue for reform. Federal pensions have been the subject of numerous studies by various federal agencies, Congress and several presidential commissions. Consequently, the retirement policies of the civil service and military systems as well as the major staff plans have been examined from various perspectives, ranging from the adequacy of benefits to the consistency of benefit design with organizational objectives.

---

1 A study is currently under way by the Labor Department to devise an approach for evaluating the total compensation between federal and private workers. However, no similar studies are planned for employees of state and local governments where the establishment of equivalent guidelines would be equally useful.

Until recently, the analysis of state and local retirement systems has been spotty. The large number of plans with widely diverse provisions has discouraged investigators from comprehensive studies of state and local systems. However, the emergence of high pension costs which threaten the fiscal stability of several states and municipalities has generated public concern and motivated both private and government research in this area.

A number of private studies have helped to identify the characteristics of the typical state-local plan and have developed analytical frameworks for approaching the major issues in the public pension field.[2] However, due to the expense and difficulty of data collection, it was not until the release of the *Pension Task Force Report* in 1978 that a comprehensive data base on state and local plans has been available. At this point, therefore, virtually all information on benefit levels for state-local government workers has been documented.

Additional information, however, would be quite useful before public pension benefits were changed. Specifically, data would be required in the following areas.

(1) Are private-sector pension plans a desirable model on which to base the design of public plans?

(2) What role do pensions play in attracting and retaining high-caliber personnel into government employment?

(3) Would the decrease in total compensation for public employees that results from a reduction in pension benefits lead to a decline in the quality of public services?

(4) Would the older workforce resulting from delayed retirement be able to provide the same level of public services?

(5) What are the tradeoffs between fewer promotional opportunities in the public sector and a larger retired dependent population?

(6) What is the incidence of pension benefits in the public sector? Are the costs actually borne by workers through lower wage growth as economists hypothesize for workers in the private sector? If all pension costs are ultimately borne by the workers, is the differentiation between employee- and employer-financed benefits a valid distinction?

INADEQUATE FUNDING, LACK OF FIDUCIARY RESPONSIBILITY, POOR MANAGEMENT OF ASSETS

The high cost of benefits has become increasingly evident as the pension systems mature and the number of beneficiaries expands. Inadequate prefunding of pension benefits has enabled previous public officials to shift the onus of financing forward to the next generation of taxpayers. The implied escalation in tax rates to finance

---

2   The most comprehensive study was prepared by Robert Tilove, *Public Employee Pension Funds* (New York: Columbia University Press, 1976).

benefits has generated considerable resentment among taxpayers who have begun to demonstrate increasing resistance to tax hikes, particularly at the state and local levels. In some cases, the situation threatens the financial stability of state or municipal governments.

The impact of inadequate prefunding is exacerbated by poor financial management of state and local pension funds. Although the trend toward consolidation of plans has resulted in greater use of professional management services, many smaller plans are administered by relatively unsophisticated part-time administrators, elected officials and employee representatives who are frequently responsible for plan investments. The natural consequence of relatively inactive financial management is unnecessary capital losses and otherwise inexplicable low returns.

The absence of fiduciary standards or guidelines for personal conduct increases the opportunity for conflict of interest or at least poor investment decision making. Where explicit investment guidelines do exist, they may be unnecessarily restrictive. For example, many states and municipalities require investments be made locally. Unfortunately, parochial interests frequently force pension trusts to forgo more lucrative investments offered in a broader market and limit the diversification of a plan's portfolio. Legislative requirements for investment in tax-free municipals can only be explained as an effort to benefit the governmental unit at the expense of plan participants and taxpayers. Since tax-free bonds have lower yields than taxable securities of similar risk, tax-exempt trusts are forced to forgo the maximum return on these investments. The consequence of poor investment management is higher costs to the taxpayers.

Options

There are several options available for improving the financial condition of public plans.

Option 1: Require periodic and frequent actuarial valuations of all public plans on dynamic assumptions in order to determine realistic future costs.

Option 2: Increase funding requirements at the federal level,[3] and through PERISA-type legislation institute funding standards for state and local plans.

Option 3: Minimize conflicts of interest at the state and local levels by establishing fiduciary standards for managers of state-local funds.

Information

While a great deal of information exists on the finances of public plans, it is not of consistent quality. The financial data for federal plans are considerably better than those for plans at the state-local levels.

---

3   True funding of federal plans would require the establishment of trust funds outside the unified budget.

Numerous federal agencies perform actuarial valuations. Civil service and the military do their own, while major staff programs either perform their own or engage the assistance of federal actuaries from major departments, such as Treasury. As a result, figures are available for most major systems.

However, inconsistency in statutory requirements for valuations has resulted in a wide variation in the frequency with which such analyses are performed for the different systems. This, coupled with lack of uniformity in actuarial methods and definitions, undermines the usefulness of the availabe data for interplan comparison or aggregation. As a result, the magnitude of the financial problems confronting federal pensions cannot be known with certainty.

Legislation standardizing actuarial methods and establishing minimum valuation intervals so that consistent data are available for all systems for a common year would make interplan cost-benefit comparisons possible and would provide precise figures on the aggregate pension financial picture at the federal level.

The seriousness of the financial data problem at the federal level is mitigated by the availability of comprehensive data and cooperative actuaries for the two largest programs: civil service and the military. Although the military system has no statutory obligation to perform actuarial analyses, annual valuations are performed by an in-house actuarial staff for internal use. Since their system is computerized, the military can respond to requests for actuarial valuations on any set of assumptions. Thus, it is possible to obtain data consistent with assumptions used by other federal plans. The civil service actuaries also produce valuations on a variety of economic assumptions in addition to the static assumptions mandated by statute.

More serious problems exist in the availability of data on the financial status of state and local plans. Infrequent actuarial valuations as well as lack of uniformity in actuarial concepts and methods make comparisons between systems very difficult and aggregation impossible. Moreover, unsophisticated administration of plans impedes the collection of reliable data on payrolls and benefit accruals for many of the smaller plans where no actuarial valuations are available. The lack of uniform financial information for state and local plans makes it difficult to isolate specific financial problems. Clarification requires the establishment of some standards for financial record keeping and actuarial valuation in order to introduce a common framework for all state and local retirement systems.

Furthermore, several basic questions must be addressed before reform is possible.

(1) What is the federal government's current authority in the regulation of public plans (particularly state and local)?

(2) What constitutes an adequately funded plan, and how do these requirements vary among federal, state, local, and private plans?

(3) What are "realistic" actuarial assumptions, and should plans be required to perform at least one valuation on a set of standard economic assumptions?

(4) What would be the impact of increased funding on: a. the fiscal status of state and local governments; and b. national saving and capital accumulation?

(5) Should state and local plans meet current plan qualification requirements under the Internal Revenue Code? Should new qualification requirements, specifically tailored to state and local plans, be designed?

(6) What conflicts of interest currently exist in the management of state-local plans?

(7) What are employees' rights in terms of the control of pension fund management? To the extent that a significant portion of assets represents employee contributions, should employees participate more actively in investment decisions?

LACK OF PORTABILITY AND COORDINATION

The absence of full portability within various levels of government exposes workers to gaps in coverage and results in double dipping.

Options

Some possibilities for dealing with these problems include the following.

Option 1: Introduce either a uniform federal retirement system for all federal workers or a full exchange of pension credits among all federal programs.

Option 2: Create a central pension fund to ensure portability for all public and private workers as they move between government and private employment.

Option 3: Guarantee all workers portability of basic pension rights through extension of social security coverage.

Information

At the federal level, detailed information exists on the portability arrangements between the various public plans. Comparable information on portability at the state-local levels, however, is not currently available. In addition, further data are required in the following areas.

(1) What is the value of benefits lost by workers due to lack of portability?

(2) What are the characteristics of employees who forfeit benefits?

(3) By how much does inflation erode benefits in the absence of the transfer of credits from one pension plan to another?

(4) Greater portability would probably increase costs—by how much and who would pay?

(5) Would portability of pension rights enhance the movement of well-qualified public managers and professionals between units and levels of government?

BENEFITS FOR HAZARDOUS EMPLOYMENT

In order to maintain a vigorous and physically qualified workforce, the military and police and fire plans provide benefits for retirement at early ages. This makes the total value of these pension benefits very expensive and considerably more generous than those provided by other public pension plans. At the same time, plans for uniformed personnel have extremely long vesting periods so that, as in the case of the military, workers who leave before completing 20 years of service receive no benefits at all.

Options

The early retirement provisions and long vesting periods for the uniformed services represent two of the areas most in need of review. Some possibilities include the following.

Option 1: Allow early retirement with delayed benefits and provide job training in preparation for a second career.

Option 2: Differentiate between hazardous and routine jobs through higher wages, relying less on pension benefits.

Option 3: Reduce vesting requirements so that those who leave before 20 years receive partial benefits.

Information

The military system has been studied extensively, and numerous proposals have been put forth to reform the program. Considerably less information is available at the state and local levels. However, for both types of plans, some very basic questions remain unanswered.

(1) How important are the pension benefits in recruiting qualified personnel into the various uniformed services?

(2) What labor market opportunities are available or could be made available through retraining to those who leave hazardous employment between ages 40 to 50?

(3) How will the goal of a youthful workforce be affected by the changing age structure of the population?

(4) What is the required age composition of a police and fire-fighting force? How many workers are involved in arduous physical activities compared to the number handling routine office duties?

PROBLEMS ARISING FROM LACK OF UNIVERSAL SOCIAL SECURITY COVERAGE

Federal civil service employees and approximately 30 percent of state-local workers—primarily police and fire fighters—are not covered by social security. Some excluded public employees profit from the progressivity of the social security benefit structure by gaining minimum coverage through brief private-sector employment while other excluded workers are exposed to serious gaps in protection. Universal coverage would eliminate these problems, but mandatory extension of social security is strongly opposed by public employees and their unions.

Options

A sample of the possible changes includes the following.

Option 1: Continue to reduce those provisions of the social security benefit structure, such as the minimum benefit, which provide substantial windfalls to short-service workers.

Option 2: Allow excluded employees to stay outside social security, but institute an exchange of credit system so that they no longer gain from the progressive benefits.

Option 3: Legislate mandatory coverage of all public employees.

Information

The issue of social security coverage differs fundamentally from the previous problems in that the nature of the problems and the theoretical solutions have been described in some detail. However, development of any practical and workable scheme for universal social security coverage would require several studies including the following.

(1) Resolution of the legal issue concerning the federal government's right to levy taxes on states and localities.

(2) Development of a detailed integration plan for civil service employees to assure workers that they will fare approximately as well under the combined programs as they currently do under civil service.

(3) Documentation of those cases where public employees have been disadvantaged by lack of social security coverage.

(4) Preparation of a study revealing the negative impact on low-income workers of solving the public employee problem by revising the social security benefit structure.

(5) Public education on the financial health of the social security system as a result of the 1977 Amendments.

(6) Presentation by the Social Security Administration of the high cost to states and localities of duplicating the entire social security benefit package.

CONCLUSIONS

On the basis of the extensive studies in the area of public employee pensions, the major problems are now identified: early retirement ages, imprudent financial planning in some state and local jurisdictions, and poor coordination among the plans of a single government unit and between some public plans and social security. Some of the contributing forces are also readily identifiable: employee pressure often unbalanced by taxpayer resistance due to the deferred nature of the cost, lack of accountability, and a multiplicity of independent government plans.

Congress has become increasingly aware of the problems with public employee pensions. Passage of ERISA in 1974 has generated considerable legislative interest in structuring similar regulations to correct abuses and provide guidelines for pension development in the public sector. In fact, the extensive study undertaken by the House Pension Task Force was mandated by ERISA to provide the necessary background information for consideration of similar legislation for government plans. Whether the federal government should introduce ERISA-like standards in the public sector is still being debated.

Although no consensus has emerged on the appropriate funding standards, the first steps have already been taken toward regulation of other aspects of state-local plans. A bill sponsored in the House of Representatives by John Dent and John Erlenborn proposes the establishment of a single Employee Benefits Agency to regulate the reporting, disclosure and fiduciary standards of state and local as well as private pensions.

At the same time, Congress has devoted considerable attention to introducing greater uniformity into the federal retirement systems. A study is now beginning to provide consistent actuarial valuations for all major federal systems. In addition, the desirability of a uniform retirement system is under consideration. These activities are supplemented by a newly commissioned President's Commission on Pension Policy which will examine the gaps and inconsistencies in the present system and evaluate the desirability of introducing the proposed uniform retirement system for all federal employees. Reform of the federal programs would naturally serve as a much needed model for state and local plans.

Universal social security coverage was considered in the debate preceding the 1977 Amendments to the Social Security Act, but a decision has been deferred pending the results of a two-year study by an independent task force. Noncovered workers as well as civil service and some state and local government workers do not receive pension benefits which are commensurate with others. Many believe that these workers' needs should be addressed immediately.

The issue of public-employee pensions is vast, complex and in need of thoughtful and serious attention not only from policy makers but also from taxpayers, both those covered by these pension systems and all other citizens. However, that attention will be random and ineffective unless questions raised in this study are answered through research and analysis. Although studies have multiplied, there are gaps to be covered and greater depth to be reached through an urgent extension of these efforts in the directions identified in this report. The necessary corrective action will only flow from public understanding leading to public demand. The thoughts recorded here are intended to contribute significantly to that understanding and to motivate the informed forces seeking changes.

National Planning Association

NPA is an independent, private, nonprofit, nonpolitical organization that carries on research and policy formulation in the public interest. NPA was founded during the great depression of the 1930s when conflicts among the major economic groups— business, farmers, labor—threatened to paralyze national decision making on the critical issues confronting American society. It was dedicated, in the words of its statement of purpose, to the task "of getting [these] diverse groups to work together . . . to narrow areas of controversy and broaden areas of agreement . . . [and] to provide on specific problems concrete programs for action planned in the best traditions of a functioning democracy." Such democratic planning, NPA believes, involves the development of effective governmental and private policies and programs not only by official agencies but also through the independent initiative and cooperation of the main private-sector groups concerned. And, to preserve and strengthen American political and economic democracy, the necessary government actions have to be consistent with, and stimulate the support of, a dynamic private sector.

NPA brings together influential and knowledgeable leaders from business, labor, agriculture, and the applied and academic professions to serve on policy committees. These committees identify emerging problems confronting the nation at home and abroad and seek to develop and agree upon policies and programs for coping with them. The research and writing for these committees are provided by NPA's professional staff and, as required, by outside experts.

In addition, NPA's professional staff undertakes research designed to provide data and ideas for policy makers and planners in government and the private sector. These activities include the preparation on a regular basis of economic and demographic projections for the national economy, regions, states, and metropolitan areas; the development of program planning and evaluation techniques; research on national goals and priorities; planning studies for welfare and dependency problems, employment and manpower needs, education, medical care, environmental protection, energy, and other economic and social problems confronting American society; and analyses and forecasts of changing national and international realities and their implications for U.S. policies. In developing its staff capabilities, NPA has increasingly emphasized two related qualifications—the interdisciplinary knowledge required to understand the complex nature of many real-life problems, and the ability to bridge the gap between the theoretical or highly technical research of the universities and other professional institutions and the practical needs of policy makers and planners in government and the private sector.

All NPA reports have been authorized for publication in accordance with procedures laid down by the Board of Trustees. Such action does not imply agreement by NPA Board or committee members with all that is contained therein unless such endorsement is specifically stated.

Recent NPA Publications

NPA Reports

Pensions for Public Employees, by Alicia H. Munnell, in collaboration with Ann M. Connolly (128 pp, July 1979, $7.00), NPA #171.

Agricultural Transportation: The National Policy Issues, by James Krzyminski (32 pp, Oct. 1978, $2.00), NPA #166.

The Role of Private Pensions in Maintaining Living Standards in Retirement, by Robert Clark (64 pp, Oct. 1977, $3.50), NPA #154.

Improvements in the Quality of Life: Estimates of Possibilities in the United States, 1974-1983, by Nestor E. Terleckyj (130 pp, second printing, October 1977, $15.00), NPA #142.

International Relations

Tales of Two City-States: The Development Progress of Hong Kong and Singapore, by Theodore Geiger and Frances M. Geiger (260 pp, second printing 1979, $7.00), DP #3.

Inflation Is a Social Malady, by Carl E. Beigie (92 pp, March 1979, $4.00), BN #24, NPA #164.

Bilateral Relations in an Uncertain World Context: Canada-U.S. Relations, a Staff Report (111 pp, Nov. 1978, $4.00), CAC #46, NPA #165.

Safer Nuclear Power Initiatives: A Call for Canada-U.S. Action, A Statement by the Canadian-American Committee (20 pp, Nov. 1978, $1.00), CAC #45, NPA #163.

Electricity across the Border: The U.S.-Canadian Experience, by Mark Perlgut (72 pp, Nov. 1978, $4.00), CAC #47, NPA #167.

A Positive Approach to the International Economic Order, Part I: Trade & Structural Adjustment, by Alasdair MacBean (81 pp, Oct. 1978, $3.00), BN #23, NPA #162.

Research and Development as a Determinant of U.S. International Competitiveness, by Rachel McCulloch (60 pp, Oct. 1978, $3.00), CIR #5, NPA #161.

Welfare and Efficiency: Their Interactions in Western Europe and Implications for International Economic Relations, by Theodore Geiger, assisted by Frances M. Geiger (160 pp, Oct. 1978, $7.00), CIR #4, NPA #160.

The GATT Negotiations 1973-79: The Closing Stage, by Sidney Golt and **A Policy Statement by the British-North American Committee** (70 pp, May 1978, $3.00), BN #22, NPA #159.

Uranium, Nuclear Power, and Canada-U.S. Energy Relations, by Hugh C. McIntyre (80 pp, April 1978, $4.00), CAC #44, NPA #158.

Also Available from the National Planning Association

NPA Membership is $30.00 per year, tax deductible. In addition to NPA reports and *New International Realities,* members also receive *Looking Ahead & Projection Highlights,* a periodical published four times per year. NPA members, upon request, may obtain a 30 percent discount on all additional purchases of NPA publications.

New International Realities, published three times a year, is a periodical written by staff members of NPA's International Division and outside experts. It is available through NPA membership or by separate subscription @ $5.00 per year. Individual copy price is $1.75.

A complete list of publications will be provided upon request. Quantity discounts are given. Please address all orders and inquiries about publications to:

NATIONAL PLANNING ASSOCIATION
Publications Distribution Department
1606 New Hampshire Avenue, N.W.
Washington, D.C. 20009 (202) 265–7685

LIBRARY OF DAVIDSON COLLEGE

Books on regular loan may be checked out for **two weeks.** Books must be presented at the Circulation Desk in order to be renewed.

A fine is charged after date due.

Special books are subject to special regulations at the discretion of the library staff.